Young Adult Library
Services Association
a division of the
American Library Association

Being a Teen Library Services Advocate

Linda W. Braun

D1502096

Neal-Schuman
An imprint of the American Library Association
Chicago 2012

Published in cooperation with the Young Adult Library Services Association.

Printed in the United States of America
16 15 14 13 12   5 4 3 2 1

Extensive effort has gone into ensuring the reliability of the information in this book; however, the publisher makes no warranty, express or implied, with respect to the material contained herein.

ISBNs: 978-1-55570-795-8 (paper); 978-1-55570-850-4 (PDF)

Library of Congress Cataloging-in-Publication Data
Braun, Linda W.
    Being a teen library services advocate : a YALSA guide / Linda W. Braun.
        p. cm.
    Includes bibliographical references and index.
    ISBN 978-1-55570-795-8
    1. Libraries and teenagers—United States. 2. Young adults' libraries—United States. 3. Young adult services librarians—United States. 4. Libraries and community—United States. 5. Social advocacy—United States. I. Young Adult Library Services Association. II. Title.

Z718.5.B67 2012
027.62'6—dc23

                                                                2012015103

Cover design by Rosemary Holderby, Cole Design & Production
Text design in Bodoni and Univers Condensed by UB Communications

♾ This paper meets the requirements of ANSI/NISO Z39.48-1992 (Permanence of Paper).

Contents

Foreword

As the economy has taken a nosedive and funding dollars have dried up or become incredibly scarce, frontline library staff have learned that they have to not only continue to develop exemplary library programs and services but also define and defend these services to funders, board members, administrators, and stakeholders. Teen services staff often have the passion and dedication for serving teenagers but limited knowledge about how to fight for access; win support from the people who pay the bills; create a campaign to educate local, state, and national government about why libraries matter for teens in their communities; and engage teens in the advocacy process. I can definitely say that these topics were not covered when I was a graduate student in library school, but over the years as I have moved from a frontline staff member to a system coordinator and behind-the-scenes administrator, these duties have been added on to my current duties as "other duties as assigned." And it's not just me who has to serve as a library advocate in my community, but all teen-serving library staff who must know how to answer the question, "What is advocacy and how does it apply to my role as a library staff member serving teens?" This is where *Being a Teen Library Services Advocate* comes in handy, from defining advocacy to instructing staff on how to be an effective day-to-day advocate to developing a long-term library teen services advocacy initiative that involves teen patrons.

I had the good fortune to be a member of the YALSA Board of Directors under the presidential leadership of author Linda W. Braun in 2009, and one of the most important things I learned from her is that successful library advocates take risks, engage teens as part of the advocacy process, and stand up for the high-quality programs and services that all teens throughout the country deserve from their local libraries. In many circles

Linda is known as the "teens and technology guru," but after reading this book I am sure that you will agree with me that she has certainly earned the additional title of "teen advocacy guru."

Michele Gorman
Author, *Connecting Young Adults and Libraries:*
A How-To-Do-It Manual
Teen Services Coordinator, Charlotte Mecklenburg Library
Editor, Teens at the Library Series

Preface

When I started out in libraries, being an advocate for any type of services, including those for teens, was the last thing on my mind. I was going to be a librarian because I was interested in working with youth and liked connecting young people to materials. As I spent increasingly more time in the profession, and in particular working with teens, I learned that if teens were going to be respected and served effectively in libraries, those librarians who worked with the age group had to stand up and be heard.

Now, being an advocate isn't something that comes naturally to me. It took some courage, some confidence building, reading and research, and networking to gain the skills and self-assurance required. As an advocate for teens, and for teen library services, I can say that the time, energy, and chances I took, and the mistakes I made, to be an advocate were (and continue to be) well worth it.

Why was and is it worth it? Part of the answer is because teens are a segment of the population that is often underserved and misunderstood. Even though there are close to 42 million teens in the United States (U.S. Census Bureau, 2012), because the age group can seem frightening and can be problematic to engage with, adults often decide to either consider all teens as bad seeds, or focus only on those teens who are well suited to traditional library services. For example, teens who like to read, will sit fairly quietly with a book, and don't make any waves (or noise) in the library.

There are hundreds and hundreds of teens in our communities who don't fit the "nice teen" model and those teens need to be served by libraries. How can we simply ignore this huge part of the population? We can't! When working with librarians who don't feel comfortable, for whatever reason, providing service to teens who are seen as "nice" and/or teens who are seen as not so nice, it's up to those of us who do value all teens to advocate for the need for service for all members of the age group. (See Chapter 1 for more on why it's important to advocate for teens and teen library services.)

What's in This Guide?

Being a Teen Library Services Advocate: A YALSA Guide is designed to help the librarian who is just learning how to be an advocate for teens to get started. Read on to find out what's included.

Chapter 1, "Understanding Advocacy by Being a Teen Library Advocate," is an introduction to teen advocacy. Advocacy is a word that is used all the time, but unfortunately it's not always used correctly. Some people confuse advocacy with marketing; they are not the same thing. This chapter covers exactly what advocacy is and what advocacy efforts are meant to accomplish. It also covers why librarians—even those not directly working in teen services—need to stand up and speak up for young adults.

Chapter 2, "Collaborations Make for Successful Advocacy Efforts," asserts that no one should have to go it alone when it comes to advocating for teens and teen library services. Realistically the only way to be really successful in an advocacy activity is to collaborate with others in the library and in the community. This chapter looks at why community collaborations are an important component of library teen services advocacy. It also looks at how to build effective advocacy collaborations.

Standing up and speaking out for teens should become a part of the daily experience of librarians. Chapter 3, "Advocating Every Day," recognizes that not all librarians are skilled at advocating on a daily basis. Some aren't prepared with a message and others don't feel comfortable speaking up for teens with colleagues and members of the community. This chapter looks at what it takes to advocate for teens 24/7, the barriers one might face in day-to-day teen services advocacy, and how to gain confidence in being a teen advocate 365 days of the year.

Chapter 4, "Go for It with an Advocacy Campaign," shows that there are times when it's important to develop a full-fledged campaign to effectively advocate for teens. In this chapter readers learn what an advocacy initiative (or campaign) looks like. It covers how to use technology in an advocacy campaign and how to gain administrator buy-in with this kind of endeavor.

Chapter 5, "Teens as Library Advocates," highlights the benefits to working with teens to enable them to become library advocates. Not only does involvement in library advocacy efforts help teens to grow up successfully, it also provides community members with the opportunity to see teens as positive members of the community in which they live. This is the focus of this chapter.

Chapter 6, "Going Beyond Your Library: State, Regional, and National Advocacy," shows you where to go next! Being a local advocate is a great first step in supporting teens and teen library services. It's also useful to think about getting involved in opportunities that give those serving teens in libraries a larger stage for speaking up and out. In this chapter readers learn why going beyond local advocacy efforts is important and find out how to get started in moving into the state, regional, and/or national library advocacy arena.

Being a Teen Library Services Advocate: A YALSA Guide ends with Chapter 7, "Tools for Being a Strong Advocate," which includes checklists and resource lists that provide the reader with the tools needed to speak up and speak out as a teen library services advocate.

As mentioned earlier, and as noted throughout this volume, advocacy can be scary. Add to this the fact that sometimes advocacy efforts aren't successful. However, the only way to make sure that teens around the country have the services they need is to advocate, and that means people have to be willing to take risks, make mistakes, and stand up and speak out for this age group. This includes all librarians, those who work with teens directly and those who do not.

Being a Teen Library Services Advocate: A YALSA Guide gives every librarian the information required to get started in advocating for teens. As a result they will improve library services, the value of the library in the community, and the lives of young adults.

Reference

U.S. Census Bureau. 2012. "Table 7: Resident Population by Sex and Age: 1980 to 2010." In *Statistical Abstract of the United States: 2012*. U.S. Census Bureau. http://www.census.gov/compendia/statab/2012/tables/12s0007.pdf.

Acknowledgments

Everything I know about advocacy I learned by being mentored by librarians, educators, and other professionals, and by being given opportunities to take risks. Thanks to those who have given me those chances, including YALSA staff, leadership, and members. Thanks, too, to all the library directors whom I've worked for and with. Even when the work experience was difficult, I learned a lot about how to speak up for teens and teen services.

To all those others working to support teens and making sure they get the services they need to grow up successfully, thanks to you, too.

Michele Gorman has been patient and helpful during the process of writing this book. Thanks, Michele.

1

Understanding Advocacy by Being a Teen Library Advocate

Imagine a man-on-the-street interview where a library reporter walks up to you and asks which of three scenarios you think provides the best example of a teen librarian advocacy effort. Which would you select?

1. A teen librarian goes to every library board of trustees meeting and listens to the discussion.

2. A teen librarian goes to every library board of trustees meeting, hands out flyers on programs, and every few months talks about the programs for teens sponsored by the library.

3. A teen librarian goes to every library board of trustees meeting and at three to four meetings (at least) during a year presents information on why teen services are important and how the activities of the library's teen services staff are helping teens develop successfully.

Did you select scenario #3 as the best example of a teen-oriented library advocacy activity? That's the one. Here's why:

- In scenario #1 the teen librarian does not provide any information to the library trustees about teen services. Her presence at the meeting helps guarantee that the trustees know that she is a staff member, but her presence does not help inform the group about why teen services are important.

- Scenario #2 does show the teen librarian as an active participant in at least some trustee meetings. However, handing out flyers and talking about programs is not really an advocacy endeavor. It's a marketing endeavor because it doesn't speak to the value of the services; it only focuses on the fact that services exist.

- With scenario #3 the teen librarian speaks to why teen services are important. Because several times during the year she addresses the value of services to teens, and how teen library services support successful growth into adulthood, she shows that the library isn't simply focused on fun and books. She explains why teen services are more than that. That's what an advocate does; she stands up for something and explains the value of what she is standing up for to garner support.

What Is Advocacy Anyway?

To put it simply, advocacy is about standing up, speaking out, and asking for support, which is what the librarian in scenario #3 does. That imagined librarian knows the importance of going beyond publicizing activities to explaining their value to a particular audience or community.

Often people mistake marketing for advocacy because marketing does get the word out about library activities. Advocacy can overlap marketing and public relations when a program or service is mentioned within an advocacy initiative, or when a program or service helps people in a community better understand and begin to support that program or service. Frequently librarians think that by marketing what they do they are advocating for what they do. This makes it seem like everyone is a teen advocate, when it's not true at all. Think about the fact that many people in the community may know about the summer reading program you have for teens. They may have seen flyers, web content, newspaper articles, and so on, but this doesn't mean they understand the worth of that program in relation to teen literacy and developmental growth. It certainly doesn't mean they support that program. Helping people to move from knowing about an activity (via marketing) to supporting that activity (via advocacy endeavors) is a key component of advocacy efforts. Take a look at the Marketing or Advocacy sidebar (pp. 3–4) to check your understanding of the differences between the two.

Marketing or Advocacy: You Decide

For each item, determine whether the activity is a marketing activity, an advocacy activity, or a combination of the two. You can also include the reason for your decision. See Chapter 7 for the answer key and more information.

1. The library website features information about teen library programs that includes the date and time and a short description. Is this:

   ❑ Marketing   ❑ Both

   ❑ Advocacy   ❑ Neither

   Why did you make that selection?

   _____

   _____

   _____

   _____

2. The director of the library mentions at a meeting of town managers that the library is collecting information and data on the need for a teen-only space in the library. Is this:

   ❑ Marketing   ❑ Both

   ❑ Advocacy   ❑ Neither

   Why did you make that selection?

   _____

   _____

   _____

   _____

3. The teen librarian speaks at a high school PTA meeting about the library collection for teens. She discusses what's in the collection, why different types of materials are purchased, and how the materials help teens to grow up successfully. Is this:

   ❑ Marketing   ❑ Both

   ❑ Advocacy   ❑ Neither

(Continued)

Marketing or Advocacy: You Decide *(Continued)*

3. *(Continued)*

Why did you make that selection?

_____

_____

_____

_____

4. A group of teens is talking about the fun they have when taking part in library programs. Is this:

❏ Marketing ❏ Both

❏ Advocacy ❏ Neither

Why did you make that selection?

_____

_____

_____

_____

5. The mayor meets with members of the press with an update on various activities going on in community departments and agencies. He mentions that the library is expanding their technology access for teens and includes information on why this access will support transliteracy skills. Is this:

❏ Marketing ❏ Both

❏ Advocacy ❏ Neither

Why did you make that selection?

_____

_____

_____

_____

What Is an Advocate?

If advocacy encompasses standing up, speaking out, and asking for support, an advocate is the person who does that standing, speaking, and asking. People often advocate for a cause in which they believe. For example, they advocate for an animal rescue league or they advocate for a political belief. They might do this by going to a rally or by speaking to local or national groups about the importance of the work of people dedicated to a particular topic. The Learning about Advocacy sidebar (see below) provides an example of how Save the Children harnessed the interest of people throughout the United States to advocate for federal funding for children's health initiatives.

Learning about Advocacy from Those Outside of Libraries

Many nonprofit organizations take on advocacy efforts to gain support for a cause and the work of the organization. For example, a Save the Children and Ad Council campaign called "See Where the Good Goes" focuses on "mobiliz(ing) citizen action in the U.S. to help local health workers help save more children worldwide" (Save the Children Federation, 2011). Since the campaign is about informing citizens about child health worldwide, while at the same time getting people involved in helping improve child health, one aspect of the advocacy effort was "Tweet Your Legislator." This campaign made it easy for anyone to get involved in making sure funds dedicated to child health would not be cut from the federal budget. By using Twitter and the web, Save the Children and the Ad Council combined key advocacy techniques to inform the public about the importance of child health, gain support, and turn support into action. Turning support into action is a great opportunity for advocacy success. As a result, this effort by Save the Children and the Ad Council proves to be a good model for exploring what advocacy is all about. (Read more about working with community members and organizations to turn support into action in Chapter 2.)

In the world of libraries an advocate is someone who is willing to ask for support for the library. Advocates ask for support for libraries in the academic community, a school community, or a town or city. A library advocate might write letters to community officials to inform them of the value of the library. Or, an advocate might speak to groups about why the library needs community support.

When it comes to teen services, an advocate is someone who speaks up and asks for support for library initiatives specifically related to young adults. This might take the form of going to each and every board of trustees meeting and making sure that members of the group are acutely aware of why teens need to be served by libraries. Or, it might take the form of getting on the agenda of a city council meeting and talking about why teens need libraries.

A key aspect of the work of an advocate is willingness to speak out, to all different types of groups, about the value of the topic for which they are advocating. When it comes to teen librarianship that means being able and willing to talk to members of the community one-on-one about why teen services are important *and* it means speaking up in larger arenas, from meetings of a specific library's governing group, to local and national governance groups and funding agencies.

What Does It Take to Be a Successful Advocate?

Successful teen library advocates acquire skills and abilities so that they can stand up, speak out, and garner support. Some of these skills may be easier to acquire than others, and for those starting out as advocates it's important to assess personal skills and abilities and know what areas one needs to work on to gain the skills necessary to accomplish an advocacy goal. A successful young adult library advocate needs to:

- Have a deep understanding of the benefits of teen services in libraries. This goes beyond what members of a community see visually as teen services, for example programs, materials, librarians, etc., to really knowing why having those programs, materials, and librarians are valuable to teens.

- Be able to articulate understanding of teen library service topics succinctly and clearly. For example, you might know very well why teen library services are key to acquisition of the 40 Developmental Assets® for Adolescents (see Chapter 7). If you can't articulate what you know to library staff, administration, governing officials, and so on, your knowledge isn't going to help you advocate successfully.

- Understand how to articulate the same ideas in different ways to different people and groups. For example, when talking to colleagues in the library you need to think about what is going to resonate with them when you talk about the way the library helps teens gain developmental assets. What will resonate with fellow staff members is probably not going to resonate with the mayor of your town. Different conversations need to take place with different audiences.

- Be a storyteller and a story collector. This goes along with the previous bullet point. Statistics have their purpose in advocacy efforts, but along with statistics it's important to be able to demonstrate value through real-life stories. It's also important to have those stories in a back pocket to pull out the right story for a current advocacy opportunity. Keeping track of what happens with teens as a result of library programs and services is required to have stories that can be told on a moment's notice.

- Know how to use different tools to keep community members up-to-date on the important work that you do and the value that it has for teens. E-mail, blogs, Twitter, Facebook, and other social media technologies are useful for getting the word out as a part of an advocacy effort. If you post regularly on these tools about what you do and why you do it, then members of the community will be more likely to remember what library teen services are all about.

- Be flexible and spontaneous. Imagine that your boss contacts you and says, "I have someone from the local education foundation here and we are talking about how the foundation might support teen services. Can you meet us in my office in 15 minutes and explain why teen services support the formal learning of young adults?" In this example, you have 15 minutes to prepare; that's not much time. Of course that means you need to have stories ready, statistics available, and clarity of message in order to speak up for teen services to a potential funder.

- Know when what you are planning is a marketing activity or advocacy activity. Putting out flyers letting people know about a library program is not advocacy. It is marketing because you are selling a program or service. Using information about that program as a way to explain how it helps to change the lives of teens is advocacy. Don't think just because you are advertising programs and services for teens that you are advocating for the age group.

Being an Advocate Seems Time-Consuming, a Lot of Work, and Pretty Scary

It's true that anyone who is successful in advocacy efforts has to commit to the activity and has to take time to prepare and gain the skills needed for success. It's also true that speaking up to anyone, from colleagues, to a city council member, to a leader of a community foundation, can be scary. And, it's true that one of the reasons that librarians of all types don't get involved in advocacy efforts is because of the barriers of time, workload, and fear. But, with practice and experience, all of the barriers can fade away. A key reason to get past the barriers is the fact that if teen librarians don't advocate for teen library services, and teens in general, then adolescents will lose out and will miss out on opportunities to gain skills and assets that are important to life success.

Getting Past Barriers

Time is a definite barrier to getting into advocacy work. So, too, is administrative support, funding, and confidence. If these barriers do exist, how do librarians serving teens get past them?

- If one of the barriers you face in getting started or even continuing in advocacy efforts is time, then take a close look at how you spend your hours at work. Consider what you spend time on and if there are any activities that you don't need to do anymore, which you only do because they are basically matters of habit, or activities that you actually could easily give to someone else to complete. Think, too, if there are ways to change how you accomplish certain tasks to open up some time. Most important, ask yourself what is the result if you don't spend time on advocacy activities that will bring in more support for teens in the community? By not taking part in an advocacy effort are you serving teens less successfully than you should? If so, then you'll want to find the time to stand up and speak out.

- When administrators or other colleagues put barriers in the way of your work on teen-related advocacy, start small and find ways to demonstrate to others in the library how your advocacy efforts won't just improve how teens are served but will help the library overall. When you present your advocacy plans to administrators and staff, remember to talk about the ways in which your goals will lead to better service for everyone and might even provide opportunities for other staff members to increase various levels of support.

- If funding is a barrier to working on an advocacy effort, consider ways in which you can start the effort with no up-front monetary costs. Also consider ways in which you can use technology and collaborate with others to advocate successfully. For example, take a look at social media and how you might employ YouTube, Facebook, Twitter, and other related tools to achieve an advocacy goal. Take a look at library departments and organizations in the community that have a goal similar to the one you want to achieve with your own advocacy activity. Encourage others to join you in the endeavor. You can pool a variety of resources, including time and money, by working together.

Why Teen Librarians Need to Be Advocates

Often, community members look at teens as the age group to avoid. Teens are seen as scary, dangerous, unpredictable, and an age group that will "grow out of it." Because of these attitudes, it's important to have people in every community who are willing to speak up and explain that teens are much more than their outer shell and much more than the assumptions that people often make about them. Because teen librarians are tasked to work with the age group, it's natural that this group of library staff members should take a central role in speaking up for them. Ask yourself who in the library:

- Knows, through one-on-one interactions, the academic and personal needs of teens?

- Is aware of the social behaviors of teens and why these behaviors are exhibited?

- Knows what is going on in the area of teen popular culture?
- Talks to teens every day about their lives and information needs?
- Keeps up with materials being published for young adults?
- Reads professional literature about library programs and services for adolescents?

Although in many libraries staff members outside of the young adult realm might know about and have experience in some of the areas listed above, it's very likely that the only staff at a library that supports teens in all of the ways mentioned in the previous list are those labeled as teen librarians. If this is the case, then of course the teen staff are the only ones who have the full complement of skills and knowledge required in order to be leaders in teen library services advocacy initiatives.

This doesn't mean that other members of the library staff should not get involved in teen-related advocacy efforts. The opposite is actually true. Staff members from a wide range of departments should be included in these advocacy endeavors, and this might occur in a variety of ways. For example, reference and adult services staff might work with teen services staff to develop talking points for conversations with non-parental adults in the community. This is a perfect collaboration opportunity. Reference and adult services staff have the information and skills required to understand the best way to present information to non-parental adults. Teen staff have information related to the points that need to be discussed with the specific audience. These staff members can develop a much stronger advocacy effort working together than when working individually.

Not only are advocacy endeavors stronger when staff members from different departments work together, but through these collaborations teen staff have many opportunities to inform colleagues of the value of serving young adults. Actually, one side goal of many advocacy efforts related to teens is to help colleagues better understand and appreciate the value of teens and teen library services.

Goals of Teen Library Advocates

For any advocacy effort it's important to know what the goals of the activity are and how it's possible to know if those goals are met. Possible goals you might want to reach as a part of advocacy efforts include increasing the following:

- Understanding of all library staff of the value of teens in the community—both inside and outside of the library
- Space, hours, staffing, and funding for teen library activities
- Access to current technologies, from hardware and devices to social media
- Outreach that allows for meeting teens where they are outside of the physical library space
- Professional development opportunities to enable teen services and other staff to be better versed in providing high-quality services to young adults
- The value placed on the importance of libraries as a central part of the life of a community
- The level of interest in library teen service by a wide variety of members of the community
- The number of people talking about the value of teens and teen library services
- Coverage in local, regional, and even national media of teens and teen services
- The ability to innovate and make change in the library and the community

One thing to keep in mind is that at the heart of all teen-related advocacy efforts is a need for the audience to understand teens and not just libraries. While you might have a very specific library goal in mind for an advocacy effort, somewhere within that goal will also have to be the increased understanding of teens (the first bullet point in the previous list). If members of the community don't understand who teens are and why they exhibit specific behaviors as a part of adolescence, it's impossible to sell the idea that library services are an integral way of supporting teen development and growth. By integrating this information and message into each bit of advocacy work that you take on, you'll help guarantee that teens are respected both inside and outside of the library.

I'm In, So How Do I Get Started Gaining the Skills I Need?

As mentioned earlier, it's important for those taking on an advocate role to assess their own skills to determine their abilities as a teen advocate (see Chapter 7, pp. 91–92, for a skills checklist). The following list provides some ideas for how to gain skills that might be required:

- **Read.** It's likely that if you are reading this book you are a librarian or educator who works at least in part with teens. Within the education and library professions there is a wide array of resources available about topics that you need to understand in order to advocate for teens and libraries. Take a look at the Advocacy Resources in Chapter 7 (p. 93) and get started reading up on the topics in which you need to learn more.

- **Talk to others.** There's no reason to work alone when developing advocacy skills. Get started by talking to others about the advocacy efforts they've been involved in, what was successful, and what wasn't so successful. Talk about what you are thinking about advocating for and get advice and support.

- **Work with a buddy.** Find someone else in your area who is also interested in getting started as a teen library services advocate. Brainstorm with this buddy the best ways to go about getting the skills needed in order to advocate effectively, work on pitches together, consider the different messages that need to go out based on audience, and practice your advocacy pitches with each other.

- **Practice.** Don't assume that just because you know the developmental assets and why they are important, you will be ready to talk about them to those from whom you are seeking support. Instead, sit down and outline or write out what you want to cover in an advocacy endeavor. Think about the audience for your conversation and what they would be most likely to consider important when learning about teen services at the library. Research whom you are going to be talking to so that you know the best way to connect with them. Don't leave anything to surprise. Then practice your talking points several times. Make sure to practice on at least one other person and ask him or her to try to listen in the role of the person who you are expecting to talk with.

- **Collect stories.** At least once a week take time to consider the different activities you, teens, your colleagues, etc., were involved in at the library in the past few days. Think about the events that could be turned into stories that will help you to gain support for teen services. Talk with others about what they experienced with teens recently and consider how those stories can connect with a particular potential or current advocacy effort. Create a collection of stories either in a database, a blog, a spreadsheet, or even a traditional notebook. Tag and/or categorize the stories so you can easily access them when you have a particular advocacy project or need.

- **Don't be afraid.** Of course this is easier said than done, but don't let fear stop you from advocacy efforts on behalf of teens. It's likely that you are passionate about the importance of teen library services and that passion can help you to move past the fear you might feel. Most people are scared when they first set out as a teen advocate, but one of the only ways to get past the fear is to have experience that leads to confidence.

- **Know mistakes are okay.** In his book *Where Good Ideas Come From*, Steven B. Johnson (2010) talks about how error is an important aspect of innovation. If you make a mistake in your advocacy endeavor, if you don't get the support you wanted and hoped for, don't give up. Take a look at what didn't work and why. Then revise. Use the mistake as a chance to learn how to do better next time. (See the next section for information on evaluating and revising advocacy efforts.)

Important to all of your advocacy skill-building endeavors is to remember to cut yourself some slack. Being a successful advocate takes time. Don't expect that you'll be perfect your first time out. Advocates who are successful in what they do are always thinking about and learning new ways to get their messages across. Know that you'll always be looking at your advocacy efforts with an eye to change and improvement. This is actually one of the reasons advocacy is so exciting to be involved in. Just like working with teens, advocacy efforts can be filled with surprises, and methods for success can change over time. Advocacy is not a static activity, just like teens are not static human beings.

I've Tried It, So Now What?

> In advocacy, well-designed efforts often fail, scaled-up efforts often
> have no more success than smaller ones, and replication of previously
> successful models doesn't always lead to success. (Teles and Schmitt,
> 2011: 8)

You've made it through your first advocacy effort. Did it work? How do you
know? Do you need to rethink what you did in order to try again at a near or
far future time? If you were to do it again, what would you have to change?
Is it really over, or is the effort just taking a break while the audience
thinks over what they've learned and you'll get back to them when the
right amount of time has passed? All of these are questions you should
ask yourself in relation to the advocacy activities that you embark on.
(Even if you have been a part of hundreds of advocacy campaigns, you can
always learn something by evaluating what happened with what you just
completed.)

Some questions to ask when evaluating an advocacy activity:

- What outcomes have I seen related to the goals that I set?
- Did I see signs that the effort spoke to the target audience(s) in the
  way that was required?
- What am I sure worked really well?
- What do I know did not work at all?
- How well did collaborations that were a part of the activity work?
- In what ways were the collaborations not so successful?
- Did we use the right tools to get the message out and inform the
  target audience(s)? If so, what worked? If not, why not?
- What kind of media coverage were we able to get?
- What do I need to do next?
- Do I need to do any follow-up? If so, what? If so, when?
- If I were to do this again, what would I change?

After answering the questions, spend some time analyzing what your
answers tell you about what you need to do next, how you need to improve
your advocacy skills, how you want to work better with other library staff

and community members, what you now understand about what it takes to be successful as an advocate, and what you want to advocate for next. It's likely that some mistakes happened during the advocacy activity. And, it's likely that at least one thing can be changed to do a better job in your next advocacy endeavor.

In the next chapters of this book you'll learn more about how to be a successful advocate and how to put together collaborations and initiatives to stand up, speak out, and gain support for teen library services.

References

Johnson, Steven B. 2010. *Where Good Ideas Come From.* New York: Riverhead Books.

Save the Children Federation. 2011. "See Where the Good Goes." Save the Children Federation. http://www.goodgoes.org/our-campaign.

Teles, Steven, and Mark Schmitt. 2011. "The Elusive Craft of Evaluating Advocacy." The William and Flora Hewlett Foundation. http://www.hewlett.org/uploads/documents/Elusive_Craft.pdf.

2

Collaborations Make for Successful Advocacy Efforts

Collaboration: Librarians talk about it all the time. Talking and doing are two very different things. Often, when people think they are collaborating they are simply cooperating. Cooperation and collaboration are not the same. Collaboration takes time and can be messy. Yet, when successful, collaboration can help build relationships, save time, and lead to benefits that go beyond what was originally intended. In the teen library advocacy arena, collaboration helps teen services staff champion their work and helps cooperating organizations and agencies better understand the role of libraries and teen library services.

What Is Collaboration?

Before going into detail about the why and how of collaboration in teen library advocacy, it's important to specifically consider what collaboration is. Collaboration is literally working on a project together. Consider a group of four people working to develop a menu for a restaurant. In this context a collaborative experience is one in which the group of people brainstorm possibilities for the menu. All members of the group throw out ideas. Each person responds to the different ideas and uses them as jumping-off points for his or her own thoughts and suggestions. Personal and professional experience is a part of the process, as each member of the team uses his or her specific background and knowledge in the idea-generation process. At the end of the brainstorming, it's not really possible to tell one person's idea from another. What is developed is a melding of what was discussed. The four people truly collaborated in the development of the menu.

On the other hand, if the menu was developed as a cooperative experience between the same four people, one person would develop the menu, the other three would make suggestions and perhaps provide some ideas for resources and changes. For the most part, however, the menu would be very much made up of one individual group member's ideas and suggestions. Melding and literally working together is not a part of the process.

Moving to the library context, when teen services staff collaborate with colleagues and community-based agencies, the staff is required to do more than respond to a few e-mails. Instead of the menu example, consider a collaboration in the development of a grant proposal that, if funded, provides opportunities to the library and youth-serving agencies in the community to advocate for teens. A cooperative process would be one in which one member of the project team writes the grant proposal and others provide feedback on that proposal. Cooperation might also come by way of letters of support.

A collaborative process for that grant proposal would be that library staff and community agency staff meet together to talk about the proposal and what they hope to achieve with it. Then they work on writing the proposal together, each adding content, revising content, and so on. It's not possible in the grant application to tell who came up with which idea. It's a seamless proposal that focuses on the needs of teens and not the needs of a particular agency or group.

Why allot so much space to describe what collaboration is? The reason is that the only way to be successful in collaborative relationships is to understand what it takes to truly participate in a collaboration, whether it's one that's advocacy-focused or one that's focused in a different area. Collaboration is not simply a word on a piece of paper. It's hard work, and as mentioned above, can be time-consuming and messy.

If It's So Much Work, Why Do It?

It might not sound like fun to take on advocacy-focused collaborations when they can be messy, labor-intensive, and time-consuming. The value, however, can't be beat. When you collaborate in teen-related advocacy efforts, you:

- Advocate simply by being a part of the collaboration. How? By explaining the value of teen services to teens and the community at every possible opportunity. By demonstrating that as a teen-focused librarian you are smart, community-focused, willing to work hard, and a key player in the area of teen development.

- Get to know others in the community with whom you can work in the future. Sometimes librarians speak a lot to one another but don't venture out to talk with others in the community. Collaborating on advocacy efforts helps to involve teen librarians in projects that aren't just library-focused and library-driven. The teen services staff member then becomes known in the community as someone worth talking with about all teen-related projects in the community.

- Get out of the library. While it can be difficult to get outside of the building, doing so makes it possible to do a better job when serving teens. By going to where colleague collaborators are, you can see what the work and world of those collaborators is really like. As a result it's possible to get a better idea of what it takes to work together successfully. Think about how beneficial it is to visit other libraries to see how things are done. The same principle holds true for visiting collaborators in their own setting.

- Gain expertise where you might not have it. Perhaps it's important for you to advocate for improved access to web technologies in the teen area of the library. Although you might recognize the need for this access within the framework of teen development, you might not be as up on the technology itself and what it takes to provide access (beyond having devices or computers available). Collaborating with those in the community who have the knowledge you lack helps you to learn and to make the case more strongly for what's needed.

- Save time. This might seem impossible since sometimes doing something yourself is the quickest way to complete a task. In the long run, working with others on an advocacy project gives you the chance to harness the capabilities of others. It might seem to take longer than if you did it yourself, but because you are not seeking out information on your own, or writing that whole report on your own, you ultimately save time. At first collaborations can take more time, because it takes time to learn how to work together successfully, but the result is

Using Technology in Collaborative Advocacy Endeavors

Different projects require different technologies. The following are some tools to consider using when collaborating with others.

From Google

Google has a variety of tools that aid in collaborative endeavors. One to consider is Google Docs, which groups can use to collaborate on a variety of text-based documents. For example, suppose you are working collaboratively on a proposal to bring to the library board of trustees. The collaborative group can use Google Docs to draft and revise the proposal. Different group members can add and edit content and it's possible to insert comments and have discussions within a document as a part of the content development. Multiple people can also work on a Google Doc at the same time, thereby making it possible to work together synchronously when not in the same location.

Google Calendar is another useful tool for collaborative activities. Calendars can be shared with small or large groups of people so that anyone can add dates and times for meetings, project deadlines, and so on. It's possible to search Google Calendar to locate specific project tasks and deadlines as well as color-code activities. Color-coding can be very useful as a way to assign tasks or organize tasks by theme. For example, red on Google Calendar may highlight meetings, whereas green events might be used for activities related to project outreach.

Google Hangouts is a part of Google's Google+ service. Hangouts are a way to have real-time video meetings. The quality of the audio and video is good and Hangouts can be used in conjunction with Google Docs so that collaborators can discuss a document in real-time using audio and video and make changes during the Hangout session. It's also possible to share a computer screen during a Google+ Hangout. If one collaborator has a diagram, document, website, etc., that she would like to show the others, she can access it on her computer, share her screen with the others, and go over the file while in a real-time Hangout.

Google+ also allows for small group (called Circles in Google+) streamed discussions. Members of the collaborative group can post ideas and comments

(Continued)

Using Technology in Collaborative Advocacy Endeavors *(Continued)*

in the stream made up of just those in the collaborative circle. Anyone in the circle can respond to the comment, add another idea, and so on.

Evernote

Evernote is a web- and app-based tool that can serve a variety of purposes for a collaborative group. Because the program is available for devices as well as on the web, it's easy to use on a device during a meeting and then synch the files created during the meeting to the web account. Then access to the files can be provided to those involved in the collaboration. The product is filled with features that can help in managing collaborative work and when exchanging information between members of a group. For example:

- A group can create what's called a Notebook, which can act as the location for holding a variety of project materials including notes, webpages, and more.
- The basic notes feature enables quick creation of task and punch lists in Evernote and these can be shared with group members. As group members complete tasks they can cross them off the Evernote-hosted list or add notes about the status of a particular item.
- Webpages can be added to the app so that when articles of interest are uncovered by group members, they can be shared, providing a quick and easy-to-use bibliography.
- Image uploading is perfect for visually focused projects; for example, for a project that focuses on advocating for improved teen spaces throughout the community, collaborative group members may take photos of furniture, color swatches, and so on and upload them to Evernote for viewing by others on the team.

Dropbox

If the collaborative group needs to share Word, PowerPoint, or many other types of files, Dropbox is an effective solution for making sure that everyone has access to the most recent version of a file. Dropbox is free (for under 2 GB of space) and works on computers and on tablets and smartphones. Another benefit to the

(Continued)

Using Technology in Collaborative Advocacy Endeavors *(Continued)*

service is that any files that are too big to send via e-mail can be uploaded to a Dropbox account and easily accessed by anyone with an invitation to the folder in which the file(s) lives. Audio, PowerPoint, and video files can very easily get to be too big to send by e-mail. Dropbox therefore comes to the rescue.

---

one that not only is high quality but takes less time to make all the necessary connections for the advocacy effort.

Collaborations don't just have to take place in traditional face-to-face settings; using technology to enhance and expand collaborative efforts is often a smart way to go. Technology can actually save time, particularly when you can use technology instead of traveling to and from an outside meeting location. See the Using Technology sidebar (pp. 20–22) for more information.

What to Collaborate On and Whom to Collaborate With

It may be easy for those working in teen services to come up with ways to collaborate on advocacy efforts that focus primarily on reading-related topics, for example, advocating for more funding for materials budgets or improving the breadth of the teen collection to include what some may consider controversial materials. It might not be as easy to advocate for topics that are less traditional within teen services. As mentioned previously, collaboration can help you to gain the expertise that you might not have on your own. It's likely that anything you want to advocate for within a teen services construct can benefit from a collaborative endeavor. Technology, space, collections, a strong teen-services program, and so on, all have a better chance to succeed if you bring others into the advocacy endeavor.

If every advocacy effort is a collaborative one, then it's extremely important that you match each initiative with just the right collaborators. The Successful Collaborations sidebar (pp. 23–24) provides some information on what makes collaboration work, but beyond that you want to think about who in the

Successful Collaborations

In order to be successful in any kind of collaboration, the people involved:

- **Need to trust each other.** In the words of Larry Prusak (2011), author of "The One Thing That Makes Collaboration Work": "If I had to pick the one thing to get right about any collaborative effort, I would choose trust. Yes, trust. More than incentives, technology, roles, missions, or structures, it is trust that makes collaboration really work. There can be collaboration without it, but it won't be very productive or sustainable in the long run." It's true, a collaboration won't work if those working together are second-guessing or even redoing the work of others. When all members of a collaborative group trust each other, then it's possible to have open conversations, plan schedules and timelines, and provide feedback and support without worry. It's important to keep in mind that trusting relationships do not happen overnight. Thinking ahead is good. Work on smaller projects with a potential collaborator in order to gain trust before going ahead with a full-fledged, advocacy-based collaborative project.

- **Commit to the effort.** The reasons that people get involved in collaborations vary and sometimes they don't have much to do with interest in the project. Make sure that those involved in your advocacy-focused collaborative efforts are committed to making the effort work. Before getting started in the collaboration, have conversations about what you want to achieve with potential collaborators. Gauge interest and knowledge. Don't think you have to bring everyone who says they are interested into a collaboration. Keep in mind the skills, interests, and knowledge of those who don't end up participating. They might fit another future project perfectly.

- **Have an open mind.** Part of what makes collaborations work is the ability to throw out ideas, even crazy out-of-the-box ideas, to see how they go over, and get feedback. Everyone in a collaborative effort needs to be open to ideas and be willing to provide critiques and responses that aren't only focused on historic practices and experiences, but leave room for the possibility that change can happen and new ways of doing things are possible.

(Continued)

Successful Collaborations *(Continued)*

- **Be good leaders.** Just because a project is being developed collaboratively doesn't mean that a leader isn't required. Consider this a project management component to the collaboration in which at least one person is responsible for helping to make sure timelines are set, goals are thought out and achieved, and communication is clear. It's possible for different collaborators to manage different pieces of the project at different times. No matter what, an organized process has to be a part of the collaboration in order to help everyone involved see there is a plan for the advocacy effort and that the plan is moving forward.

---

community—what person or organization—is best suited to the advocacy effort you are about to embark upon. Although many times it's possible to collaborate with the same people over and over again, those same people might not be best suited for a particular advocacy initiative. For example, advocacy efforts related to technology are prime opportunities to connect with IT specialists and members of the community who work in technology companies. Collection-based advocacy efforts are ripe for collaborations with bookstore owners, reading specialists, and authors. Even if you love working with the parent who is always supportive of teen services, in some instances it might just not make sense to involve her in the endeavor.

Keep in mind that even if a potential collaborator has a good knowledge of the topic for which you want to advocate, each person's point of view will have an impact on the endeavor. For example, police personnel and lawyers have a great deal of background that may come in handy when working on advocacy efforts that help members of the community understand teen behaviors and development. However, you want to make sure that those within the professions who are involved in a project as collaborators are positive supporters of teens and have stories and experience to bring that shed favorable light on the age group.

A good way to get started when coming up with the best collaboration partners is to write down the goals of the advocacy project and the skills and knowledge that you require from collaborators in order to succeed. Then think about the members of the community who have the skills, knowledge, contacts, and experience that will help you meet your goals. Try to think

Selecting Collaborators		
Activity	**Overview**	**Who Are the Potential Collaborators?**
Overall support for teen services	For this type of advocacy effort, you want to make sure to include those who have a dedicated interest in and knowledge of guaranteeing that youth in the community have the support needed to achieve success. Those involved in this activity should work with teens regularly and understand adolescent developmental stages. Some members of the group should have a strong connection to the community, be able to speak from experience in working with diverse groups in the community, and wield respect from a variety of community members.	• Adult services staff • Architect • Artist • Author • Bookstore owner • Circulation staff • College professors • Curriculum developer
Unfiltered technology access for teens	Key in selecting collaborators for this advocacy effort is including people on the team who understand teens within the context of their interest in and use of technology. In this collaboration, you also want to make sure to include those who understand technology infrastructures and laws that relate to teen use of technology in schools and libraries. Also important is an understanding of how technology can be used as a tool to expand teen access to information and provide opportunities for successful development and growth.	• Fire department personnel • Graphic designer • Health care workers • Hospital staff • Interior designer • IT specialist • Lawyer
		(Continued)

Selecting Collaborators *(Continued)*		
Activity	**Overview**	**Who Are the Potential Collaborators?**
Integration of social media in teen programs and services	For this advocacy effort it's important to make sure that those involved understand the value of social media as a tool for the informal and formal learning experiences of teens. While there may be people in the community who understand social media as a result of their own personal use, in order to send the message about its value in teen lives it will be important to have members of the team who can speak to how social tools enhance learning. These are people who understand that social media is not just about the social.	• Library administration • Literacy specialist • Marketing specialist • News reporter—TV, newspaper, web • Parent • Police personnel • Psychologist or psychiatrist
Expanded collection to include materials that some might consider controversial	Members of the community who can bring experience from the world of publishing as well as an understanding of why access to varied materials is important to teens can provide many connections and knowledge to the group working on this advocacy activity.	• Public relations specialist • Reading specialist • Religious leaders • School/public library counterpart
Increased space for teen services	This is a perfect opportunity to collaborate with architects and interior designers in the community. Along with these professionals, it's also a good idea to think about *(Column cont'd.)*	• Social service employees • Software developer
		(Continued)

Selecting Collaborators *(Continued)*		
Activity	**Overview**	**Who Are the Potential Collaborators?**
Increased space for teen services *(Continued)*	individuals who understand the psychological implications of the use of space. Also, look for those who understand what environments work best for formal learning and what work best for informal learning.	• Teacher • Technology specialist • Web developer
Increased staff for teen services	Consider individuals in the community who understand that knowledge of teen development is a requirement for supporting teens in formal and informal learning situations. Look for collaborators who can speak up about the need for teens to have mentors and role models and the value of library staff performing these roles as a part of library service.	• YA literature professor • Youth worker

outside of the box when coming up with collaborative partners for a project. Don't just think about the traditional members of the educational community that the library tends to work with. Be expansive in your thinking. Even think about how you might take a risk when developing advocacy partnerships. Is there a person, organization, or business that you have always thought the library should connect with but never had a way to do that? Perhaps this advocacy collaboration opportunity is just what you need to get started making that connection.

The Selecting Collaborators sidebar (pp. 25–27) provides a list of some of the topics for which you might advocate, along with information on what to consider when determining who to collaborate with on the advocacy effort and a list of potential collaborators from within a community. Use the ideas and list as a jumping-off point for considering who you could work with in your community on this type of effort.

Just Do It

Think about the many things you want to advocate for in teen services. What is one that you've always wanted to take on but haven't been able to find the time for, or just don't think you have the expertise to do? Your answer is very possibly a good candidate for a collaborative effort. Sit down and consider who in the community can help you to get started with the effort and who can help you put the pieces together. Start talking to them and find out what ideas they have. Before you know it, you will be collaborating on an advocacy project that could make a big difference in the lives of teens in the community.

Reference

Prusak, Larry. 2011. "The One Thing That Makes Collaboration Work." *Harvard Business Review*, July 5. http://blogs.hbr.org/cs/2011/07/one_thing_that_makes_collaboration.html.

3
Advocating Every Day

For some librarians it might seem that advocacy is something that is accomplished at very specific times for very specific purposes. That's not really the case. The best way to be a successful teen advocate is to make advocacy something you do every day. There are times that you'll work on special advocacy initiatives, but if you go beyond that and advocate every day that means that you take every opportunity to talk about the value of teen library services whenever and wherever you can. You can do this when helping parents, teachers, or others to find materials. You can do this when checking out materials to members of the community. You can do this when you are at a meeting of community members with whom you are collaborating. You can do it all the time.

Chapter 1 covered the skills and knowledge necessary to be a teen library services advocate. In this chapter you'll learn more about those skills within a day-to-day advocacy context.

A Day in the Life

What's the day in the life of a librarian who works with teens like? It includes talking with colleagues, community members, teachers, parents, teens, administrators, vendors, and more. It involves going to meetings, picking up lunch at the local sandwich shop, and spending time with teens in formal and informal programming, and involvement in general library activities. Imagine what it would be like if every activity that the teen services librarian participated in had an advocacy component. The A Day in the Life sidebar (pp. 30–35) takes you through a day in the life of a teen services staff member in which this is the case.

A Day in the Life		
Time	**Activity**	**Making the Advocacy Connection**
9:00 a.m.	Arrive at work and you see the director of the library while walking to your desk.	Making a statement as you walk by saying, "I'm so excited about the program we've got planned for later this week. Teens are going to be creating Animoto book trailer videos. And, while they do they'll get a chance to gain media literacy skills and better understand how images and text help to get a message across. They'll even learn about searching and copyright as they look for images to use in their videos. Stop by if you want to see all that in action."
9:15 a.m.	Get a phone call from a parent asking you if the book his daughter is looking for is available for picking up later in the day.	While you check the catalog to see if the title is available you say to the parent, "I read that book and was amazed how well the author demonstrated how difficult it is for teens to build trusting relationships with each other. I know a lot of people say the book is just fluff, but there is so much more to it and it's really an important part of our collection because it helps teens learn how to be caring in their peer relationships."
9:45 a.m.	It's time for you to leave for a meeting with members of a community group who are developing *(Column cont'd.)*	As you leave you stop to say "hi" to your friend who is a reference librarian. "Hi, are we still on for lunch around 1:00? I hope so because I really want to tell you how well this meeting I'm heading off to *(Column cont'd.)*
		(Continued)

A Day in the Life *(Continued)*

Time	Activity	Making the Advocacy Connection
9:45 a.m. *(Continued)*	plans for new teen space for the library.	goes. I'm so excited that this group is interested in helping plan the new teen space. We really need it. I know you know, but I just have to say, when teens have a space of their own they will be better able to recognize that the library values teens and realizes the important role the age group plays. We'll also be able to have a better chance to provide materials and collections that support their specific developmental needs. I'm so excited."
10:00 a.m. to Noon	Facilitate meeting with community members who you are working with to plan the library's new teen space.	Throughout the meeting you take the time to highlight why library teen services matter. You bring up the Search Institute's 40 Developmental Assets® for Adolescents and discuss how a space just for teens will help the age group meet the assets. You explain how a collection that is just for teens in a teen space is better able to serve the needs of the age group. You discuss how getting teens involved in the space development process helps the teens to gain a variety of skills including planning and project management.
12:30 to 1 p.m.	You get back from the meeting and have a few minutes *(Column cont'd.)*	The teen colleague's e-mail outlines all of the trouble she is having getting support for teen services in her library. *(Column cont'd.)*

(Continued)

A Day in the Life *(Continued)*

Time	Activity	Making the Advocacy Connection
12:30 to 1 p.m. *(Continued)*	to go through your e-mail before having lunch with your reference colleague. You find an e-mail from another teen librarian in the area.	You respond by suggesting that she collect stories from others in the area about how teens have benefited from teen services. You provide an example of a teen you know in your library who had a hard home life. When he first came to the library he acted out all the time and the librarians were really frustrated with him. However, you and a couple of colleagues started talking with him, found out what he was interested in, and then connected him to books and other materials that helped him learn about his interests. Now that teen is in college and excelling in all of his classes.
1:00 to 2:00 p.m.	Lunch with your friend and colleague who works in the reference department of your library.	While the two of you try very hard not to just talk about work, it's hard not to. Your friend does ask you about the meeting and you are able to report how you are helping members of the group better understand teens and the value of the library in teen lives. Your friend asks how you are doing that and you mention that you are bringing up topics such as the developmental assets. Your colleague doesn't know about the assets so you promise to send her the link when you get back to the library.

(Continued)

A Day in the Life *(Continued)*

Time	Activity	Making the Advocacy Connection
2:00 to 2:05 p.m.	You have a few minutes at your computer before you need to start working a bit on collection development and before teens come to the library after school.	You send the link to the Search Institute website and the 40 Developmental Assets to the friend you had lunch with and ask her to let you know if she has any questions or ideas.
2:05 to 3:00 p.m.	The new *VOYA* and the new *SLJ* are on your desk.	You read reviews, selecting the titles you want to add to the collection. There are some titles that you know you need to have but you also know that some people in the community might find the content questionable for the age group. As you select the materials, you make a list of these potentially controversial titles and put together an e-mail for your director that lets him know about the titles you are going to add to the collection and highlights why it's important to add them. In the e-mail you focus not on the literary quality but instead discuss what teens can learn from having the titles in the collection. You let him know to get in touch if he has questions.
3:00 to 3:30 p.m.	Teens are out of school and ready to *(Column cont'd.)*	The first teens to arrive are those who are working on planning and *(Column cont'd.)*

(Continued)

A Day in the Life *(Continued)*		
Time	**Activity**	**Making the Advocacy Connection**
3:00 to 3:30 p.m. *(Continued)*	hang out at the library.	implementing a program for the annual community spring festival event. Teens have been working on the activities the library will sponsor and they are going to contact some of the community small-business owners this afternoon to talk about how the owners might get involved in the event. Before teens start making calls, you go over the script with them that you and they developed together and talk about how to make the phone call interactions successful.
3:30 p.m.	A senior citizen who uses the library a lot sees the teens on the phone and asks what they are doing.	You talk with the senior about the teens' project and explain how the teens are gaining a variety of skills by taking such a strong leadership role in the project.
4:00 to 5:00 p.m.	You are scheduled to be the library roamer, walking through the reference and teen areas asking people if they need help.	As you walk through the library, you stop to talk with some teens who are hanging out in the library. You notice a few adults giving you and the teens some evil looks as you talk (not very loudly) to each other about various topics. As you talk with the teens, you make sure to model how to have conversations with the age group and how you help to keep the teens from getting too crazy by talking with them *(Column cont'd.)*
		(Continued)

A Day in the Life *(Continued)*		
Time	**Activity**	**Making the Advocacy Connection**
4:00 to 5:00 p.m. *(Continued)*		as human beings who have brains they can use to make good decisions. When you walk past the adults who gave you the evil looks, you say "hi" and mention how much you appreciate having the chance to show teens that you care about them and show them that adults are interested in what they have to say.
5:00 p.m.	It's time to go home.	Before you leave, you e-mail the youth commission director you talked with at the meeting earlier in the day and let him know some dates and times you are available for a conversation about youth development. You also mention how much you appreciate his mind-set related to teens and that you are very much looking forward to working with him on the current and future projects.

The eight-hour day depicted in the sidebar is pretty busy for this library staff member, and at every opportunity she advocates for teens and teen library services. She does this by:

- Reminding the library director that the programs the library sponsors for teens are not just about fun. Although she hopes that teens have a good time while attending programs, she also makes sure that she can articulate the informal and formal learning opportunities that are a part of all of the programs teens are involved in at the library.
- Taking opportunities to remind colleagues why what is going on in teen services is important to the library and to teens.

- Talking up the value of all materials in the teen collection, even those materials that might not be considered of high literary quality.

- Reminding community members about what the library is working to accomplish in its work with teens.

- Making connections to like-minded community members. She can talk to these people about teens and how to support them in the community, while at the same time educate these community members about how the library is a key player in making sure teens grow up successfully.

- Keeping the library director apprised of what the teen library collection strives to achieve and why having materials that might be of concern to some in the community is valuable to the collection because of what they provide teens.

- Modeling for community members the positive role that teens can play in the community.

- Showing teens that she cares about who they are and what they think.

What It Takes

The librarian whose day is outlined in the sidebar didn't end up as a 24/7 advocate the day she started working in libraries. It took her time to build up confidence and skills to be that type of advocate, and it took practice, and even making mistakes, to figure out what she needed to do, when, and how. What can you do to gain the skills needed to be a 24/7 advocate? Try these ideas:

- **Start small.** Think about your schedule one day during the upcoming week. What are you doing that provides tangible opportunities to be a teen services advocate? Is there a staff meeting on that day? If so, then think about a time during the meeting when you can do a bit of an advocacy push for teens. A great way to do this is to get on the agenda to talk about teen services and what you are striving to achieve that goes beyond "fun" and having quality literature on the shelves. Can you get on the agenda to talk about the programs that are coming up and how they support learning initiatives in school? Or, get on the agenda to discuss how the teen library collection supports STEM (Science, Technology, Engineering, and Mathematics)?

- **Start with once a day.** Charge yourself with integrating a day-to-day advocacy conversation at least once a day. Keep track of when in the day you take this step and what you talk about. After you find that you are doing this once a day, raise the ante to twice a day, and keep going until it's just a part of what you do on a regular basis.

- **Pay attention to what doesn't work.** If you start advocating for teens as a part of your regular daily library life, you are sure to find that sometimes the advocacy steps you take just don't work. Maybe the colleague you decided to talk to about the value of controversial literature in the teen collection didn't take well to your message. Ask yourself why that conversation didn't go well and find ways to try again using a different tactic for getting the conversation going or for keeping others engaged, interested, and positive.

- **Pay attention to what does work.** When you speak up for teens as a part of your day-to-day teen services life, look for examples of what you found to be successful. Think about why these experiences were successful and how you can replicate them in a variety of situations. While the message might not always be the same, the way it was presented is worth paying attention to in order to continue to be successful in this area.

- **Develop elevator pitches.** Since 24/7 advocacy means that you need to be ready to advocate at a moment's notice, if you develop a selection of elevator pitches that you can pull out when needed, you'll feel more confident in your ability to advocate every day. See the Ins and Outs sidebar (pp. 38–39) for more information.

- **Develop infographics.** Over the past couple of years, infographics have become a popular method for getting statistics across on a particular topic. If you have a selection of infographics available on a variety of topics that demonstrate the value of teen services you can pull them out on an as-needed basis to advocate when the opportunity arises. See the How to Use Infographics sidebar (pp. 39–41) for more information.

The Ins and Outs of the Elevator Pitch

Over the past few years the elevator pitch (selling an idea or service within the time of a traditional elevator ride) has become an often-talked-about method for getting information across to a particular audience in a short period of time. A 2007 *Business Week* article says in just a few words exactly what the value of an elevator pitch is: "Being able to sum up unique aspects of your service or product in a way that excites others should be a fundamental skill" (Pincus, 2007).

What does it take to be successful in a great elevator pitch?

- **Know that one size does not fit all.** Make sure that you have different pitches for different audiences. The topic can be the same but how you address that topic has to vary. For example, when talking with a school administrator about the value of the technology programming you do with teens, you might integrate statistics on how technology programming correlates to improved student test scores, reading skills, and so on. The same topic of an elevator pitch to colleagues might focus on how teens who take part in the technology programming provided by the library gain competencies related to social skills.

- **Write or outline first.** It might seem odd to write out an elevator pitch since the pitch is supposed to feel somewhat spontaneous. Nevertheless, it's definitely a good idea to put your pitch ideas and points on paper first. Once you have a topic that you want to be ready to talk about in a pitch, write down the key points and be aware, when you do, which audience each point is best suited to.

- **Practice.** Don't try an elevator pitch that you haven't gone over previously. Although winging it might work in some situations, getting a point across successfully in a short time requires little to no fumbling and a real dexterity in the presentation of information. This lack of word fumbling and dexterity can only come with practice.

- **Revise as needed**. Don't let your pitches get stale. Make sure to update them with new statistics, new examples, and new ideas on a fairly regular basis.

(Continued)

The Ins and Outs of the Elevator Pitch *(Continued)*

- **Pay attention.** Keep track of the times you wished you had an elevator pitch ready and make sure to work on one for that audience and purpose as soon as possible. You might not have been able to pitch at the first opportunity that arose, but next time you'll be ready.

How to Use Infographics for Library Advocacy

Several months ago I put out a question on Twitter asking members of my professional learning network how they were using infographics in their advocacy efforts. It was a little surprising to me that only one person responded with an example. Others responded by saying things like, "Oh, that's a good idea." But it looked like people weren't using infographics as a way to inform their library community about what they do and why they do it.

Then I talked with YALSA board member/strategic planning chair and high school librarian Priscille Dando about data, advocacy, and infographics and I found out that she used PowerPoint to create a visual that demonstrated the use of her library in the spring of 2010. One thing that really struck me about Priscille's infographic was that it was produced simply with PowerPoint, a tool that most (if not all) librarians have access to, and it used clip art to effectively get out the message that the high school library is an active, vital part of the school community. (You can see Priscille's infographic in the original blog post.)

Perhaps one of the reasons that more librarians aren't using infographics in order to tell their library story is because it seems like they are difficult to produce. As Priscille's visual demonstrates, it doesn't have to be a challenging activity. Along with PowerPoint and clip art there are a host of tools available for creating infographics. These include:

- **Many Eyes**—This tool from IBM gives users the chance to upload data and create visual displays for that data. Display types include charts, graphs, and word and phrase clouds. One really nice feature of Many Eyes is that when reviewing the types of visualizations, the site provides tips on what each type is best used for. For example, under the heading

(Continued)

How to Use Infographics for Library Advocacy *(Continued)*

"See Relationships Among Data Points," scatterplot, matrix chart, and network diagram are listed.

- **Creately**—This is a web-based tool (with a desktop version also available) that provides templates for a wide variety of diagrams, including some specifically geared to those in K–2 education. A good feature of Creately is that it's possible to collaborate with others when using the program for infographic building and design.

- **Wordle**—Many blog readers are familiar with Wordle and it's good to remember that this is a tool that can be used to create advocacy-based visuals for the library. Think about how you might use Wordle to display all of the ways that teens describe the library, or to show the words and phrases that come up over and over again when teens and others in the community talk about the value of library teen services. If you start to think about it, you'll see that Wordle has a lot of potential as an infographic building tool.

Along with knowing how to create infographics, it's also important to think about what data is best to use in a visual display. Not all information lends itself to this format. In her article "Ten Awesome Free Tools to Make Infographics," Angela Alcorn (2010) states, "Remember that it's all about quickly conveying the meaning behind complex data." As you look at the data and information that you want to get across to members of your community, keep this idea in mind. Ask yourself questions such as:

- Which data lends itself to a visual display?

- What data is going to best help others understand the role of library teen services within the community?

- Is there data that when shown visually in an infographic format will demonstrate an idea that can't be easily articulated in writing?

Keep in mind as well that infographics often have visual themes that help to send the message. Consider what theme you might use to get your visual data across successfully. Also remember that you want to make sure the visual display is

(Continued)

How to Use Infographics for Library Advocacy *(Continued)*

as high quality as the data. If the data isn't readable because of the colors or images used, then it has no value. This is another reason why simple is good.

There are many good resources available to learn about infographics and how to create them. Make sure to check out the links in the "10 Awesome Free Tools" article (Alcorn, 2010) to learn more.

(*Source:* Adapted from Braun, 2011.)

Going Beyond Yourself

A holy grail in 24/7 teen services advocacy is working in a setting in which the entire library staff speaks up and out for teens whenever an opportunity to do so arises. Your 24/7 advocacy will act as a model for colleagues in your library so that they have examples of how to advocate for teens on a regular basis. Often, though, your colleagues need to have more than modeling. They have to be convinced that it is worth their while and of value to the library for them to be a teen services advocate. Some ways to make that happen follow:

- **Work with your administration.** Speak up to the library administrator about the fact that teens are a library audience that interacts with all library staff, from children's services staff to adult reference staff and from circulation staff to technology staff, and that uses a wide variety of library services for their personal and educational needs. As a result, all library staff need to be able to provide high-quality service to teens and they need to be able to articulate to the community why the teen audience should be served. Make sure the library administrator is aware of YALSA's white paper (included in full in Chapter 7) on the whole-library approach to teen services, a useful tool for gaining full library advocacy support from administrators. See the What's in It for Administrators sidebar (pp. 42–44) for more information.

- **Talk about teen services** and the value those services add to the library and the community as a regular part of staff meetings. Get on the agenda for staff meetings as much as possible. Whenever you talk about teens, highlight the positive implications for development and

What's in It for Administrators?

Administrators have to think about how each department succeeds separately and how all departments working together make the library successful as a community agency. It can be hard sometimes for administrators to value discrete advocacy efforts focusing on a specific customer group as beneficial to the library as a whole. To sell teen services advocacy as something that is a win-win for teens, for the library as a whole, and for the entire community, consider how to discuss all advocacy endeavors not just as teen-focused but also as full library- and community-focused. For example:

Advocating For	How It Is a Win for Teens	How It Is a Win for the Library	How It Is a Win for the Community
Teen-only space	Teens have a place to go in the library in which their needs are specifically met. When teens visit the library, they see that they are valued as much as everyone else in the community because they have space to call their own, just like children and adults.	The library demonstrates to teens and the community that they recognize the value of teens and that they serve all members of the community from birth on.	Teens have physical community space that is available specifically for them and their needs. As a result, teens have a place to go to learn, take part in leisure activities, and hang out with friends.
Staff dedicated to teen services	Teens know that the library is a place that they can go to get their questions answered. They *(Column cont'd.)*	Every service of the library specifically developed for teens is created with an understanding of *(Column cont'd.)*	The community is supported by an agency that has the needs of teens at heart. As a *(Column cont'd.)*

(Continued)

What's in It for Administrators? *(Continued)*

Advocating For	How It Is a Win for Teens	How It Is a Win for the Library	How It Is a Win for the Community
Staff dedicated to teen services *(Continued)*	know that when they visit they will be respected. As a result, they feel supported and empowered.	the unique needs of the age group. As a result, community members see the library as a trusted place where teens are understood and are supported in their informational and leisure interests and development.	result, teens are given the support needed to be productive and positive members of the community.
Building a well-rounded collection	By providing materials on a wide range of topics, the library is giving teens access to resources that help provide answers to their questions. They gain information so that they can make smart choices about their lives.	The library is seen as a community agency that gives teens opportunities to learn how to act responsibly and make good choices.	Teens are well-informed and as a result make good decisions about how they behave as valued members of the community.
Open access to web content	When teens have open access to web content, they are given *(Column cont'd.)*	The library becomes a place that is seen by community members as helping *(Column cont'd.)*	Teens are community members that know how to *(Column cont'd.)*

(Continued)

What's in It for Administrators? *(Continued)*			
Advocating For	How It Is a Win for Teens	How It Is a Win for the Library	How It Is a Win for the Community
Open access to web content *(Continued)*	opportunities to learn how to be safe and smart with that content. As a result they are able to make good decisions when it comes to access and use of web-based materials.	teens to understand how to use technology safely and smartly. It therefore becomes a trusted educational institution for all ages.	make good decisions and are therefore able to positively participate in community activities inside and outside of school.

learning in what you do for the age group. If staff are having a hard time being positive about teens, you be the positive force that they can't ignore.

- In your daily conversations with colleagues, subtly or not so subtly **mention what you are doing with and for teens and why.** For example, if you are starting to expand teen technology access, mention this to other staff members, but don't just say, "We are going to add more laptops in the teen area." Be more specific, along the lines of: "We are going to add more laptops in the teen area. I'm so excited because this will give me the chance to work with teens even more and help them learn how to be smart and safe users of technology and specifically of social media." The *why* is a key component. Without it, staff might simply think, "Oh, sure, more computers in the teen area so that those kids can hang out on Facebook and not be productive at all."

- **Involve teens in your advocacy endeavors.** In many instances, teens talking about the value of the library in their own lives is the best way to advocate for services. Administrators, funders, elected officials, and colleagues are likely to find teen stories of library impact compelling and as a result may be more able to recognize the value of services to the age group. See Chapter 5 for more information on how to involve teens in library advocacy efforts.

Make It a Part of Your Job Description

It would be marvelous if every librarian's job description included being an advocate for teens every day. Unfortunately, many job descriptions do not cover advocacy. Don't let that stop you from taking on the role of 24/7 teen advocate. When you get to work every morning, commit to speaking up and out for teens as much as possible, with all members of the library community from colleagues and administrators to parents, teachers, seniors, and others who work in the area. Once you start, you'll find that it gets easier and easier. Once you start, you'll find that others start doing the same. Once you start, you'll take an important step in making sure that teen services are valued and understood where you work.

References

Alcorn, Angela. 2010. "10 Awesome Free Tools to Make Infographics." *MakeUseOf* (blog), October 8. http://www.makeuseof.com/tag/awesome-free-tools-infographics/.

Braun, Linda W. 2011. "30 Days of How-To #17: How-to Use Infographics for Library Advocacy." *YALSA Blog*, September 17. http://yalsa.ala.org/blog/2011/09/17/30-days-of-how-to-17-how-to-use-infographics-for-library-advocacy/.

Pincus, Aileen. 2007. "The Perfect (Elevator) Pitch." *Business Week*, June 18. http://www.businessweek.com/careers/content/jun2007/ca20070618_134959.htm.

4

Go for It
with an Advocacy Campaign

The previous chapter covered information on how to advocate for teens on a daily basis and how to incorporate advocacy into your daily work as a library staff member. Day-to-day advocacy is important, and so is determining which advocacy efforts need a bit of an extra push with a full-out advocacy initiative, or campaign. How do you decide when to go the next step and build a campaign? For that matter, what is an advocacy campaign? Read on to find out the answers.

What Is an Advocacy Campaign?

To put it simply, an advocacy campaign is when you develop and organize a focused effort to advocate for—and gain support of—a very specific initiative. When advocating 24/7, you do not usually focus on one specific area for which you want to gain support. With a campaign, you do focus on one specific area. For example, perhaps you want to gain support for creating a teen-only space in your library. You might start out discussing it with people on-the-fly to educate them about the need for the space. As your day-to-day advocacy grows for this project, you might realize that you need a plan if you want the teen-only space to see the light of day. If a more organized approach is needed, then it's time for an advocacy campaign.

The most common advocacy campaigns in libraries are those related to large-scale funding, either for a new building or in order to gain support for the institution's budget. In recent years as the United States faced an economic downturn and library budgets were often in the news for potential large cuts, librarians have built local, state, regional, and national campaigns to get out the word about the value of the library to the community.

A few of these recent advocacy campaigns are worth taking a look at to understand what might occur in, and what's required of, a teen services–focused library advocacy campaign.

- In 2010 and 2011, the Save NYC Libraries campaign worked to get out the word that the potential budget cuts for libraries in New York City (New York Public, Queens Library, and Brooklyn Public) could be devastating to New York City neighborhoods. The librarians who took the lead in these campaigns staged high-profile events to guarantee that people noticed what could be the result of large library cuts. In June 2010 the *New York Times* reported on one of the campaign events, a Read-In, in this way: "Not typically ones to raise their voices, librarians staged an overnight Read-In on the steps of the Brooklyn Public Library on Grand Army Plaza to criticize the city's plan to close 40 branches by month's end, and to reduce hours and employees at those that remain" (Grynbaum, 2010). The *New York Times* article in which this quote appeared was just one piece of media attention the Save NYC Libraries campaign received. The large-scale photo opportunity events gave the press something to talk about when it came to libraries and potential budget cuts.

- Library Snapshot Day is a project that libraries across the United States take part in to demonstrate to their communities what goes on in a library within a 24-hour period. While the name of the campaign may suggest that the focus is on photos of libraries during a day, this isn't all that it's about. Data that tells the story of how a library is used and what library staff achieve in a day is also key to the success of this campaign. It's possible that members of the community don't really know what happens in a library in a 24-hour period. Library Snapshot Day helps to rectify this, and by doing so can demonstrate to the community why the library is worth supporting and funding.

- The Marshall District Library implemented the *Geek the Library* campaign as a way to inform and educate community members about the role of the public library in the small Michigan community. Funded by the Bill and Melinda Gates Foundation and developed by OCLC, The *Geek the Library* project is a community public awareness campaign that is focused on spreading the word about public libraries and their funding needs to community members (OCLC, 2012). In Marshall, staff throughout the library were involved in the project, which helped the library to create a buzz in the community about the campaign and about the value of the library. Community members were given opportunities to get involved by being a part of the marketing and public relations efforts. As a result, not only were community members learning about the library, they also had a chance to make a difference in building awareness by being a part of the actual campaign (OCLC, 2010).

What did all of these campaigns have in common? Several things:

- **They were collaborative.** It's rare that an advocacy campaign can be successful when carried out by one person with a mission and plan. Advocacy campaigns that bring a group of people together who all have the same goal and objective are more likely to succeed (see the Collective Impact sidebar below). As mentioned in Chapter 2, collaborations can help you achieve your advocacy efforts, and this is true for smaller projects as well as larger campaigns.

What Is Collective Impact?

Chapter 2 of this book is devoted to the idea of collaboration and the important role that it plays in advocacy endeavors. However, when thinking broadly about advocacy, specifically when thinking about advocacy campaigns, it's important to recognize the potential of collective impact for long-term change in an organization and a community. John Kania and Mark Kramer (2011) define collective impact as "long-term commitments by a group of important actors from different sectors to a common agenda for solving a specific problem. Their actions are supported by a shared measurement system, mutually reinforcing activities, and ongoing communication, and are staffed by an independent backbone organization." The authors also state, "examples suggest that substantially greater progress could be made in alleviating many of our most serious and complex social problems if nonprofits, governments, businesses, and the public were brought together around a common agenda to create collective impact."

(Continued)

What Is Collective Impact? *(Continued)*

The components of successful collective impact outlined by Kania and Kramer (2011) include an agreed-upon agenda, shared measurement systems, and strong and ongoing communication. From a teen library services perspective, the authors' idea of mutually reinforcing activities provides a potential first step in library advocacy campaigns that include a collective impact piece. Mutually reinforcing activities are activities sponsored by those collaborating on a project that meet the specific mission of each organization. In addition, these activities are planned and implemented to support the activities of others in the community working toward the same goal/impact.

What's an example of a mutually reinforcing activity that might be part of an advocacy campaign related to teen services? Imagine you have started a campaign that has the goal of raising funds in order to expand the print library collection to serve a more diverse teen population. Your partners in the advocacy campaign include school librarians, the youth commission in the community, an author, a publisher, and a bookstore owner. The bookstore owner is hosting an event in which an author of YA fiction is going to speak about her latest novel. This event is a common activity for the bookstore owner. The event helps to promote the bookstore, helps to make sales for the book, and, in general, gets people interested in young adult literature. Now that the bookstore owner is involved in the library's teen collection expansion advocacy campaign, she makes a point to contact teen services staff to determine if the date for the author program fits with the library's schedule of teen programs. She works with the teen services staff to develop the publicity materials for the event. And, she gives the library staff the opportunity to speak about the library campaign as a part of the author introduction on the night of the event.

The bookstore owner and the library teen services staff work toward the same impact—enhancing teen reading of fiction. They work toward that goal separately but also together and by doing so have a much greater chance of achieving success.

- **They were led.** Even if an advocacy campaign is highly collaborative, that doesn't preclude the need to have a few leaders who are able to keep the project going. This doesn't mean that others outside of those in leadership roles aren't planning, implementing, and speaking up and out. It simply means that there are designated individuals paying attention to the details to make sure the campaign succeeds and keeps its momentum.

- **They were organized.** An advocacy campaign doesn't have a chance at success if it isn't organized. Although not every aspect of the campaign has to be mapped out in detail, the group working on the campaign should understand the goal and know what is needed to achieve that goal. Organization of the campaign can take the form of assigning roles, looking for partners, creating timelines, creating PR materials, and so on. A sense of what's going to take place and how, even if things change along the way, has to be in place when the campaign gets started.

- **They were media-oriented.** All of the campaigns listed previously created very specific opportunities for media to get involved in the campaign. Read-Ins, photo ops, and so on can draw bloggers, reporters, videographers, and more who will help get the word out. Hosting events that have media potential can lead to success.

- **They were focused.** Having a very specific goal is key in an advocacy campaign. What do you want to achieve by the time the campaign is over? It's important to be able to tell those to whom you are advocating what the goal is. Know that from the beginning.

Doing It Yourself—The Pieces

If you are going to launch an advocacy campaign, you will want to prepare to make sure you are focused, organized, media-oriented, led, and collaborative. As you prepare:

- Know your goal and what you hope to achieve by the end of the campaign. Ask yourself what you are trying to accomplish and what success will look like.

- Think about the audience you want to target for the campaign. Are you going to reach out to parents of teens only? Do you want to focus on community members generally? Who is going to receive your advocacy message and why are they the best audience for the initiative? Have those answers before you get started.

- Craft your message. The message is something that is repeated frequently during an advocacy campaign. It can be used in elevator pitches and often can be made into a slogan that is easy to remember and can be used in a variety of materials and platforms. Think about the words and phrases that best describe and get across the point of your initiative. Then work to use those repeatedly during the campaign.

- Have in mind the people who will be best to collaborate with on the campaign. Consider the goals and audience for the initiative and then develop a list of potential collaborators. Remember to think a bit outside of the box and focus not just on the tried-and-true library teen services supporters. Include individuals who aren't traditionally targeted for collaborative endeavors but who might be able to help you get your message out to your audience in order to reach your goal.

- Research and plan the strategies you might use to reach your audience and goal. This could include traditional methods such as letters to the editor and presentations at face-to-face meetings. You might also incorporate techniques that use social media and web-based tools to get your message across.

Doing It Yourself—Selling It to Administrators

If you are thinking about going the campaign route for an advocacy initiative, determine which teen services endeavors require a campaign and which ones can simply benefit from 24/7 day-to-day advocacy. Ask yourself if you need a focused campaign for general overall support for teen services in the library and the community, or if you are able to get that support through ongoing 24/7 advocacy efforts. Consider whether something that requires fundraising or a change in the library facility is worth a concerted advocacy effort. Not everything needs to be handled through a campaign, but some activities do require this focused effort in order to make a change.

If you want to put together an advocacy campaign to expand, extend, and/or improve teen library services, it's likely that you can't do so without the support of the library administration. An advocacy campaign is not something you can start without the benefit of high-level support. It certainly isn't something you can do under the radar. If you put the pieces mentioned earlier together, you'll be able to work with administrators to get their support. Along the way you'll need to:

- Be able to articulate to library administrators why a campaign is necessary. This includes articulating why the goal needs to be achieved as well as why it's important to go with a campaign as opposed to something more low-key and perhaps even more long-term.

- Inform administrators about how you are going to evaluate the impact and outcomes of your advocacy campaign to determine success and that your goal has been reached. You can do this by including measurable goals and objectives as a part of any campaign materials that you provide to administrators. For example, an end goal might be to have raised a certain amount of dollars that can be used to create a new or improved teen space.

- Have information on hand about who you can work with in this campaign. What other organizations, businesses, and community members can help you to achieve your goal? Don't forget to get some library colleagues on board with the project. Those in other departments of the library can be very helpful in implementing advocacy campaigns. Before you talk to administration, you should have at least a few people who support you in the campaign and have agreed to help out if you are able to move forward.

- Know what you want to implement as a part of the campaign. For example, if you are going to use various types of online and print media to help get the word out, you should be able to describe what your plans are for the media and PR portions of the campaign. If you plan to use social media, be able to describe what you hope to achieve with those tools.

- Be specific about the amount of time you will need to plan and implement the campaign. Be realistic about the number of hours per day or week you'll put into this effort. Consider the amount of time you'll need to take away from the library as well as the time you'll take while in the library.

- Note that the campaign is a work in progress and that while you have a plan in mind for how it will work, when it will take place, who will be involved, and so on, you might have to make changes along the way. At the same time let administrators know that you will keep them informed about how things are going and any changes you need to make that they should know about.

Doing It Yourself—Web-Based Tools

In the second decade of the twenty-first century, there are a number of opportunities to integrate virtual tools and social media to create an advocacy campaign that enables you to connect with a large number of potential supporters and to gain their support. Following are some tips on using specific social and web-based tools and examples of how the tools can be used in an advocacy campaign.

Twitter

It's possible to create a voice and a following using Twitter. It's also possible to tell your story even within the short message construct of Twitter. Make sure to create a Twitter presence specifically for your advocacy campaign. Set up a Twitter account that is just for the project and tweet from that account. Think about the profile picture used for that account and make sure it is something that helps to brand your advocacy initiative. Also, make sure others are ready and able to retweet what you post as a part of your initiative. Don't forget to create a hashtag that is specific to what you are focusing on in your campaign. The hashtag should be easy to remember. With Twitter you might:

- Report daily or weekly on news related to your advocacy campaign.
- Sponsor regular chats in which members of the community can ask questions and talk about the current advocacy campaign.
- Link to news reports and articles that highlight the value of the goals of your campaign.

Facebook

For many members of the younger population, using Facebook in advocacy efforts is a key aspect of long-term success: "The 'Survey of Young Americans' Attitudes toward Politics and Public Service' study, conducted by Knowledge

Networks in February [2011], found that 32 percent of college students with Facebook accounts believe advocating for a political position using online tools has more of an impact than advocating in-person. Twenty-seven percent of 18- to 29-year-olds surveyed said the same" (Kaye, 2011). One component of Facebook that makes it an important tool to use in some advocacy campaigns is the way in which video, photos, and text can be linked and embedded on the site's pages. Connected to the embedding capabilities of Facebook is the ease with which those who support your campaign can embed video, photos, and links that you provide into their own pages. Your library's Facebook page is not the only place where media content can live when Facebook is used.

Make sure to look into Facebook Causes as a way to create a platform for supporters to connect with your advocacy campaign. Also, consider starting a Facebook page just for the advocacy campaign. That way you can post content that won't get lost on a page that has other information about library programs and services.

With Facebook you might:

- Regularly post videos and photos that demonstrate the value of the goals you are trying to reach through your advocacy campaign. These videos can help to put a human face on the improvements to teen services you are working toward through your campaign.

- Promote discussion about videos, photos, and links posted on the Facebook page. If you post a video of teens talking about why the new space you are raising funds for will make a difference in their lives, you can ask teens and others to comment on that video and have a discussion that expands on what the video covers.

- Spread the word by helping supporters use your content on their Facebook pages. Make sure that those who are involved in your campaign—teens and adults—post videos, photos, and links related to the initiative in their own Facebook spaces. This is a very useful way to use word-of-mouth techniques for getting information out to the community.

Google Docs

There's no doubt that Google Docs is a great way to collaborate with those who are in different locations. It's probably not as often recognized that

Google Docs can be a good tool to use beyond the "getting things done" aspect of collaborations. Google Docs can be used to gather stories and crowdsource content that you might use in an advocacy campaign. If you make a Google Doc public, you can make sure that anyone who has information that might be useful to you in your campaign can add it to the Doc.

Google Docs is also a good way to demonstrate transparency in the work of those behind the campaign. If all campaign documents are public on Google Docs, it's possible to invite collaboration as a part of meeting planning and even while a meeting is going on.

Ways in which Google Docs can be integrated into an advocacy campaign include these:

- As agendas for meetings are developed, post them on Google Docs and ask others in the community to comment or make suggestions via the Google Doc commenting features. Owners of Google Docs can use the settings to allow viewers of the document to post comments without giving them the ability to edit the document.

- During meetings of the planning group, use Google Docs to take minutes and invite those who aren't at the meeting to add comments and ask questions while the meeting is going on using the Google Docs commenting features. This involvement of the community will help you to gain buy-in as everyone is given the opportunity to understand and participate in the goals and work of the project.

What to Keep in Mind in the Social and Virtual World

When planning for the integration of social media and online tools into your advocacy campaign, keep in mind the following:

- Carefully consider which tools are likely to be the most effective in meeting your goals and targeting your specific audience. There are instances when you will want to use a number of different tools to reach your audience. In other instances, one or two tools will be all you'll need.

- If you are going to use more than one technology-based tool for your advocacy initiative, keep in mind that the same techniques might not

5

Teens as Library Advocates

Previous chapters covered how to collaborate with others in the community to be successful in teen library services advocacy. Adults aren't the only community members with whom you might collaborate. Getting teens involved in advocacy efforts not only helps the library but also helps teens.

Advocate and Grow Up Successfully

The 40 Developmental Assets® for Adolescents from the Search Institute is a perfect place to start when thinking about getting teens involved in advocacy endeavors (see Chapter 7 for the complete list). The assets outline a framework for what teens need so that they grow up successfully. As the Teens as Library Advocates sidebar (pp. 60–61) shows, many of the activities that a teen would be involved in as a part of a library advocacy activity support the assets.

Getting Teens Ready to Be Library Advocates

You can't simply say to a teen, or group of teens, "Go out and advocate for the library." Before teens can advocate for teen library services, they need some training and practice. Here's what you'll need to do to prepare them:

- Have conversations about what advocacy is and why it's important for the library. Ask teens to think about times when they advocated for themselves with parents, teachers, or other adults. Have them think about techniques they've used to speak up and speak out to gain support for something they wanted or needed. Making connections to

Teens as Library Advocates and the Developmental Assets

The 40 Developmental Assets from the Search Institute provide an excellent framework for considering how library programs and services support the successful growth of young adults. The following chart takes a brief look at how providing teens with opportunities to be library advocates supports specific assets. See Chapter 7 for the complete list.

Asset	Connection to Library Advocacy Opportunities for Teens
Support	"Other adult relationships" is one of the assets listed in the developmental assets support category. When librarians spend time with teens helping the young adults gain advocacy skills, the teens and the librarian have an opportunity to build relationships that go beyond advocacy efforts and demonstrate to teens that they are supported and that adults value the age group as important members of the community.
Empowerment	Teens who are trained to be library advocates are given opportunities to be a resource in the community. They are given a useful role to play and as a result can feel as if they have the power to make a difference in the world in which they live.
Boundaries and Expectations	When teens learn to be library advocates, a portion of that learning has to focus on when it is appropriate to take a stand and when it is better to hold back. Teens, therefore, get practice at understanding boundaries; they also learn how to gauge others' expectations and plan accordingly.
Constructive Use of Time	As teens learn to be advocates for the library and set out to act as library advocates, they are spending time in constructive endeavors.

(Continued)

Teens as Library Advocates and the Developmental Assets *(Continued)*

Asset	Connection to Library Advocacy Opportunities for Teens
Commitment to Learning	To be a successful advocate for teen library services, young adults have to be immersed in learning. They learn about the library and its goals and mission. They learn about the community and what is required to successfully connect with various members of the community. They may learn about fundraising and how community politics work. And, after teens have taken part in an advocacy initiative, they need to learn how to evaluate the effort and consider revisions for the next time around.
Positive Values	Honesty, integrity, and responsibility are all traits defined by the Search Institute as a part of the positive values asset. Teens who participate in library advocacy initiatives gain all of these traits by taking the responsibility to be involved in a project of this type and speaking up about the library with honesty and integrity.
Social Competencies	A library advocacy project requires that teens work with adults and their peers. As a result, the young adults involved in the initiative will gain valuable skills related to interacting socially with others.
Positive Identity	A teen involved in a library advocacy initiative will have the opportunity to see change happen and have an impact on change that occurs. Being empowered in this way, being able to work with adults and peers on a project of import to the community, and learning how to speak up about something of interest is bound to help young adults be positive about themselves and what they are capable of.

the real lives of the teens will allow them to better understand what advocacy at an organizational level requires and is all about.

- Talk about the different ways that advocacy can take place. For example, talk with the teens about the ways in which advocacy can happen 24/7. Brainstorm with teens the ways in which they can help support the library via an everyday approach to advocacy.

- Converse about focusing advocacy efforts not just on the *what* of library teen services but also on the *why*. While teens devote a part of their advocacy efforts to talking about how much fun it is to be at the library and the kinds of programs and services provided, they will have more success if they can talk about why the library is important in their lives. Help teens to articulate the *why* by asking them what their visits to the library and participation in library activities has led to in their lives. You might ask them how the library has made a difference in their friendships and relationships. You might ask them to talk about how the library has helped in their schoolwork. These kinds of questions will help teens to better understand what they are specifically advocating for.

- Brainstorm the different tools that can be used for advocacy initiatives. Talk about how the teens might use Facebook and Twitter, YouTube and Flickr, and face-to-face meetings to help advocate for the library. (See the Using Technology sidebar in Chapter 2, pp. 20–22, for information on technology tools that can be used in collaborating on and managing advocacy efforts.) Have examples available for the teens so that they can see what others have specifically done. You and they can critique the examples with an eye toward what will work for your community and your library.

- Focus on the message. Give teens the chance to talk about what that message is and the best way to get it across to the audience. Have the teens brainstorm slogans that they might use. Also, give them a chance to write and practice elevator speeches. This is a perfect opportunity to talk with the teens about who the audience for the message is and how the way a message is presented might change based on with whom the teen is advocating. You can also talk about language and how to revise and reframe language based on the audience and the platform on which the message is going out. Teens will understand that a message going out to friends on Facebook about the library will be framed and written differently than a message going out to members of the library board of trustees, or parents, via e-mail.

- If part of the teen's advocacy efforts includes presenting at meetings, make sure to work with the teens as they develop their presentation. Help them to frame their ideas for their audience and give them opportunities to practice what they are going to say. Give teens a chance to talk about what makes a good presentation and what makes a poor presentation. They might develop criteria for a successful presentation so they can evaluate what they are working on before going out and presenting. Also, give teens practice answering questions. You can ask the teens questions that might be expected from some of the adults in the audience. This will give the teens the chance to think about their answers and help guarantee they have good answers for the types of questions adults might ask.

- Explain that advocacy doesn't always lead to success, or that success might be achieved but only in part. Make sure that the teens understand—and give them the chance to talk about—the fact that success is not guaranteed and that they might be in for a letdown. Give the teens the chance to talk about how they will feel if their efforts don't succeed and how to handle the outcome if it's not what they want or intend.

- Consider with the teens ways in which their advocacy efforts can be evaluated. Talk about how they will know if they have been successful and how they might make changes if their efforts are not as successful as they would hope. Make sure that the teens know it's okay to make mistakes and that an important part of learning is recognizing when mistakes are made and then working on ways to rectify them and make changes so that they don't happen again.

Once you've had conversations with teens and given them a chance to write, create, and practice, you'll want to continue to check in with them as they work on advocating for the library. If the advocacy effort that teens are participating in is somewhat long term (see the next section for ideas on advocacy projects in which teens might participate), you'll want to schedule regular meetings or check-ins to find out how things are going, what advocacy the teens have participated in, and any help or support they might need as they move forward.

Teen Advocacy Projects

Is every advocacy endeavor that you might be involved in something that teens can be a part of? Probably. It's likely, however, that you will want to think carefully about what aspects of your advocacy work make sense for teen involvement. The following gives some ideas of how teens might be involved in advocacy efforts:

- Present to teachers, parents, administrators, elected officials, librarians, board of trustees, community members, and so on.
- Write articles, letters, and opinion pieces for the local newspaper, the library blog, and other media outlets.
- Post on social media including Twitter and Facebook.
- Produce videos to post on YouTube and embed on their own and the library's website and social media presence.
- Take photos to post on their own and the library's social media presence.
- Create content in a variety of formats—audio, video, and text—that can be integrated into library staff advocacy presentations.
- Talk to members of the community in informal settings.
- Through their participation in library activities, model the value that the library has to their lives.

Check out the following ideas for specific advocacy projects in which teens might be involved.

The Overall Value of Teen Library Services

This is a 24/7 advocacy topic in which teen library users can easily be involved. Teens can get in the habit of mentioning their use of the library and why it's important to their lives in the conversations they have with parents, teachers, employers, librarians, and peers. Of course, most teens aren't going to do this 24/7, but getting the point across that when they have the chance it's okay to talk about the library, and how and why they use the library's services, is something you'll want to do.

Library teen advocates can also model the positive impact that libraries have on their lives while in the library. Teens who participate in library activities that give others in the community the chance to see the teens positively involved in the community can be a powerful way to demonstrate the value of teen services. Seeing is believing, and adults, colleagues, and administrators who see teens in a positive light in the library will be much more open to expanding, enhancing, and supporting teen services overall.

Creating or Enhancing Teen Space

It's possible that the best voices to speak up about the need for teen space in the library are teens. As the primary users of the space, teens know exactly why they need a library area dedicated just to them, and they know what it takes to make a library space appealing. Although librarians and other adults in the community can provide statistics and research on the importance of space in teen lives, the teens are the ones who can bring the message home through real stories about their lives and the intersection between real-life and library space.

Teens who advocate for space might speak at library board of trustees meetings about the value of a teen-specific space. They might survey their peers to gather data about what they think is lacking in the community when it comes to comfortable space for hanging out and doing schoolwork. The teens can also talk to members of the community about the difference that a library teen space will make to the adolescents who live in the community. And, they can use YouTube, Flickr, Facebook, and other social media platforms to post images and videos that show what a teen space will look like and the impact it will have on their lives.

Strong Teen-Focused Collections

In spring 2011, the #yasaves hashtag launched on Twitter. The hashtag was in direct response to an article in the *Wall Street Journal* about young adult literature and the harm that some books might bring to teen lives (Montovani, 2011). The #yasaves hashtag was a way for readers and writers of teen literature to say, "No, these books don't do harm; they do good by saving teen lives." Those who used the hashtag told stories of how YA literature had saved their own life or the life of someone they knew.

Books for teens that have dark themes, that include sexual information, that focus on sexual identity, and so on can seem scary and problematic to some adults. Teens and librarians can help to remove this fear by speaking up and out about how these books really do help teens better manage and understand their lives. In an advocacy context, teens can take the same #yasaves approach and talk with adults via social media, in blog posts, and face-to-face about the ways in which teen literature helps them to understand the world they live in. Teens might also write newspaper articles that describe the value of titles that some might find objectionable. They can speak at library board of trustees meetings, PTA meetings, and so on to get the word out that novels with themes that might make adults nervous have very positive potential.

Open Access to Technology

The ways in which libraries do and don't provide access to technology for teens is not that different from the ways in which libraries do and don't provide access to print materials. Fear can have an impact on decisions about collections and technology. When it comes to technology, some adults in the community, as well as some colleagues and administrators, fear that teens will be harmed by visiting a website, using a social media tool, or downloading content. Teens can help dispel these fears by speaking up and out about the ways in which technology is used positively in their lives. Similar to #yasaves, teens can discuss when technology has helped them to better understand their lives, succeed in relationships, and complete school-related work.

An advocacy effort in which teens work to help expand their access to technology in the library might include teen presentations and articles published in local media outlets, as mentioned previously. The teens might also teach technology classes to older or younger members of the community. While these classes aren't on the surface specifically advocacy-related activities, they provide the community with opportunities to see how teens are using technology positively. As a result, these teaching activities end up as a subtle advocacy effort that can have great impact.

State Library Legislative Day

Many librarians around the country have worked with the teens in their library to prepare them for talking with legislators at their state's library legislative day. Teen involvement in this activity brings the value of teen library services to the doorstep of legislators, who need to understand why they should support libraries and the services they provide. In a podcast on the *YALSA Blog* (Braun, 2009), Sarah Couri, a teen librarian at New York Public Library, discusses how she prepared teens for their trip to New York State's Library Legislative Day and what the teens accomplished while they were there. The blog post also includes a video, produced by Couri and the teens, in which the teens talk about the role the library plays in their lives. It is clear from the podcast and the video that before the trip to Albany (NY), and before recording the video, teens talked about the important points to get across to members of the state's legislature. The teens spoke to the *why* of teen services and not just the *what*.

Membership on the Library Board

Getting involved in library governance gives teens a good opportunity to speak up and out about the value of library teen services. Depending on the way a library's board is organized, a teen might have to stand for election to the board, he or she might have to petition to be appointed to the board, or a library might have a space specifically open on the board for a teen member. If it's not possible for someone under 21 to sit on the library board, it is likely that a community member who recently graduated from college can serve. Someone of that age who has recent experience with the library's teen services can speak to the value of those services and be a strong advocate.

A teen who sits on the library board not only can help inform other board members and administrators about the value of the library in his or her life, but it's also possible that this teen can learn more about how the library works and as a result be a better general advocate for teen services in the community. Teen board members can act as liaisons between the board, teen library staff, and teens. They can be well situated to plan and implement projects that will be appreciated and supported by the board and administrators.

Get Ideas from Teens

As you talk with teens about the advocacy initiatives and activities in which they might be involved, get their ideas about what they think they should take on and how they can help. You might think that teens will be just right for an advocacy effort, then when you talk with them learn that no, they aren't really right for it at all. Or, you might think teens won't be interested in a particular advocacy activity and then talk to them and learn that they are extremely excited about the chance to participate in that specific activity. Don't make assumptions about what teens are interested in or capable of when it comes to advocacy. Ask them to find out where the reality lies.

References

Braun, Linda. 2009. "YALSA Podcast #65—Teens Talk to NY Legislators." *YALSA Blog*, March 26. http://yalsa.ala.org/blog/2009/03/26/yalsa-podcast-65-teens-talk-to-ny-legislators/.

Montovani, Melissa. "Book Community Gets Behind #YASaves." *Examiner*, June 5. http://www.examiner.com/young-adult-fiction-in-toronto/book-community-gets-behind-yasaves.

6

Going Beyond Your Library: State, Regional, and National Advocacy

Talk about scary! Just thinking about advocating for teens and teen library services outside of the local community sometimes puts fear in the hearts of even the most successful and comfortable locally focused advocates. It shouldn't really be so fear producing. It's possible to take all the skills one uses at the local level and use them just as successfully in a broader arena. Besides, state, regional, and national advocacy isn't something you do on your own. There are many great people advocating for teens and teen services beyond your local community and you get a chance to work with them when you broaden your advocacy horizons.

Why Leave the Comfort Zone?

Let's talk about the benefits of advocating for library teen services in a large arena.

As already mentioned, advocating at the state, regional, or national level brings you in contact with many others who have the same goals and the desire to see library teen services succeed. When you connect with these other individuals, you have the chance to brainstorm ideas with those who have different and perhaps more experience than you do. They also might have had opportunities to expand their vision of teen services and teen services advocacy, which means they can help you to expand your own ideas and give you a chance to think about libraries and teens in new ways.

While working on advocacy in your own local community is important, when you expand to a larger stage you have the opportunity to help guarantee that teens throughout your area, or throughout the United States, have the same resources and support that you are making sure are available in your own community. Let's face it, teens everywhere need the support that you are advocating for locally. How else are you going to make sure that they get it unless you go out and speak up to a larger audience?

It is important to demonstrate to those in your local community that this issue is of state, regional, and national importance. By going outside the local community to advocate for teen library services, you actually might be more successful at the local level. It's one thing for teen services staff members to talk about how valuable the services are at home. But to show that what you've been passionate about locally is something that is also recognized at a broader level, and that your passion extends outside of the local community, can convince some to buy in to the value of your advocacy efforts.

Are There Challenges?

Yes, there are different, or even more, challenges when advocating on a larger stage than when you stay focused on your local community. Advocating at the state, regional, or national level might mean that you need to go to meetings and other events that take place during your regularly scheduled work hours. If this is the case, then you will want to talk to your administrators about the value of what you are doing, why it is beneficial to your own library, and how you will be able to keep up with your day job while advocating outside of the library. If it's not possible to be away from your library to participate in broader advocacy activities, there are ways to get involved that do not require events outside of the library. The Broad-Arena Advocacy sidebar (pp. 71–72) provides some ideas.

Another challenge is finding the right type of large-arena advocacy endeavor that suits your particular interests and needs. How do you know what's the best one or ones for you? See the How to Make Decisions sidebar (pp. 73–74) for criteria to use when making choices related to advocacy efforts that take place outside of your own community.

Broad-Arena Advocacy without Leaving Home

Even if you can't leave your library for advocacy activities that go beyond your local community, it is possible to get involved at a broader level. Consider some of the following options to get yourself started.

Send

Many library and teen-focused organizations send out alerts when state or national legislation is in the works that could have an impact on library services, and in general, services that have an impact on youth. Get on the mailing lists, Facebook pages, or Twitter feeds for the state, regional, and national organizations that have a connection to teens and teen library services and pay attention to the alerts that ask you to get in touch with a state or national government official. ALA has several tools you can use to keep up with library-related legislative news. Visit the ALA Washington Office website (http://www.ala.org/ala/aboutala/offices/wo/index.cfm) for more information. Send those letters, tweets, and e-mails that are requested to make sure that your voice is heard and that you are a part of the work being done to support teens.

Post

It's possible to make your voice heard on teen issues by posting in a variety of venues that reach a broader audience than your local community. Get yourself blogging for YALSA or another organization that has an advocacy focus. You can then post about the importance of speaking up and out for teen library services. Use Twitter and Facebook as a venue for speaking up about the value of teen library services. You can use these social media tools to post information about advocacy campaigns of import to those serving teens in libraries and to generally inform about the *why* of teen library services and their value to adolescents. Keep in mind if you do start posting professionally on social media that you want to make sure to consult with your library administration about your institution's social media policy.

Create

Even if you can't go to an event at which people are going to talk about the value of teen library services, you can still create content for that setting. Why not put

(Continued)

Broad-Arena Advocacy without Leaving Home *(Continued)*

together a video with the teens in your library that you post on YouTube and that highlights the value of teen services? The video could be played at the event so that your voice and ideas are heard. You can also create infographics, which can be discussed at the event, that show the impact of teen library services on teen lives. Collaborate with others in your state, your region, or nationally to collect data on a topic related to the value of teen library services and then make your point about that data with an infographic. (See the How to Use Infographics sidebar in Chapter 3, pp. 39–41, for more information on infographics and how to make them.)

Map

In March 2010, school librarian Shonda Briscoe created a Google Map that helped to visually demonstrate what the impact would be when cuts to school library funding were made (Valenza, 2010). Librarians around the United States added their schools to the map and wrote about what was happening with their community's school library funding. As Wendy Stephens wrote in a Twitter post in October 2011, "Nation Without School Libraries map by Shonda Brisco—each dot is 1or 2 librarians, but thousands of students" (http://twitter.com/wsstephens). Maps of this type can be used in a host of ways to advocate for teen library services. Why not be a part of a Google Map that shows how libraries around the country are improving teen interest in reading through book discussion groups? Or why not get involved with librarians around the country who put information on a Google Map that shows how their programs support STEM? By creating and participating in these maps, it's possible to demonstrate visually the potential for and power of teen library services.

You might need to learn about how your library defines advocacy and make sure that those you work with understand the goal of your advocacy activities when working from a larger stage. There are times when library staff, administrators, and trustees worry that advocating is the same as lobbying, and in some institutions lobbying is not allowed. Talk with your administrators about what you will be doing when advocating at the state, regional, or national level. The Advocacy and Lobbying sidebar (pp. 75–76) provides you with some talking points and information to get started in those conversations.

How to Make Decisions about Large-Arena Advocacy Endeavors

Use the following self-assessment when deciding what advocacy activities to get involved in at the state, regional, or national level.

1. Where do your passions lie when it comes to advocating for library teen services? What do you like to speak up and out about? (Check all that apply.)

❏ Programming   ❏ Space

❏ Collections   ❏ Technology

❏ Funding   ❏ Teen Services in the Whole Library

❏ Adolescent Development   ❏ Other—Explain: _____

2. What types of advocacy activities do you like to get involved with? (Check all that apply.)

❏ Writing about the value of teen library services

❏ Presenting to groups about the value of teen library services

❏ Creating content (videos, etc.) that helps to demonstrate the value of teen library services

❏ Being a part of planning related to teen library services

❏ Collaborating with those outside of the library world on teen library service advocacy projects

❏ Collaborating with those in the library field on projects related to advocating for teen library services

❏ Working with teens on projects that help to advocate for the value of teen library services.

❏ Other—Explain: _____

3. Approximately how much time can you give to a broad-arena advocacy effort?

❏ 4 or less hours a month (approximately one hour a week)

❏ More than 5 hours a month (approximately 2 or more hours a week)

❏ Other—Explain: _____

(Continued)

How to Make Decisions about Large-Arena Advocacy Endeavors *(Continued)*

4. Are you able to participate in advocacy efforts that take you outside of the library during your normally scheduled work hours?

   ❏ Yes   ❏ No

5. Are you already involved with any groups that make it a part of their mission to advocate for teens?

   ❏ Yes   ❏ No

6. If yes, what are those groups? (Consider state, regional, and national library, education, and youth groups.)

   _____

   _____

   _____

7. If you were to contact a group to get involved in teen services–related advocacy efforts, what skills would you say you have that you could bring to the work of the group?

   _____

   _____

   _____

8. Consider your answers above and in the space below write a few sentences about what the information tells you about what you are looking for in a state, regional, or national advocacy effort. Then use the paragraph as a way to match your interests, skills, and abilities with the different opportunities that are available. Look for opportunities that match your passions, interests, time available to devote to the effort, and so on.

   _____

   _____

   _____

   _____

Advocacy and Lobbying: What's the Difference?

Frequently I talk with librarians about advocacy in teen services. We talk about what it means to be an advocate. We talk about how to get started in advocacy efforts. We talk about how to find time to advocate. We talk about a lot more related to speaking up and out about teen services to a variety of audiences including colleagues, community members, and government officials.

I recently realized that for some librarians there is a concern that if they talk with government officials—legislators and such—in order to advocate for teen services, that they might actually be lobbying. And, for some, lobbying is not allowed within their job description. This got me thinking, what is the difference between advocacy and lobbying?

First I read the *Wikipedia* article on lobbying that includes this definition (that comes from *Merriam-Webster* and *BBC News*):

> "Lobbying" (also "Lobby") is a form of advocacy with the intention of influencing decisions made by the government by individuals or more usually by Lobby groups; it includes all attempts to influence legislators and officials, whether by other legislators, constituents, or organized groups. (http://en.wikipedia.org/wiki/Lobbying)

After reading that definition I thought, okay, the influence part is an important piece of the lobbying definition. Then I read about the difference between advocacy and lobbying in a document from the Connecticut Association of Nonprofits (2003). In their advocacy/lobbying toolkit they include this statement:

> Although most people use the words interchangeably, there is a distinction between advocacy and lobbying that is helpful to understand. When nonprofit organizations advocate on their own behalf, they seek to affect some aspect of society, whether they appeal to individuals about their behavior, employers about their rules, or the government about its laws. Lobbying refers specifically to advocacy efforts that attempt to influence legislation. This distinction is helpful to keep in mind because it means that laws limiting the lobbying done by nonprofit organizations do not govern other advocacy activities.

(Continued)

Advocacy and Lobbying:
What's the Difference? *(Continued)*

What this means to librarians working with teens who wonder if they can talk to legislators at an event like library legislative day, or even in the community if a legislator is at a local event, is yes, even if your employer's policies state that you are not supposed to lobby as a part of your job, you can go to something like a library legislative day and advocate for teen library services.

You can advocate by speaking up and out to *educate* legislative officials about the value of teen services in the community. You can speak up and out to *educate* about the need for teen space in libraries. You can speak up and out to *educate* about the role that technology plays in teen lives. You can speak up and out to *educate*. You just can't exert influence in order to have a legislator vote a particular way on a particular piece of legislation.

Advocacy is such an important aspect of what librarians do in their work with and for teens that it would be unfortunate if it was left behind because of a misunderstanding about what is and isn't allowed. If you are not allowed to lobby as a part of your job, talk with your administrators about the differences between advocacy and lobbying. You probably do want to make sure that you are clear, and that your administrator is clear as well, what those differences are. Then go out and advocate whenever and wherever you can.

Don't let the no-lobbying portion of your organization's policies (if it is a portion of those policies) keep you from advocating in order to educate and inform. It's an important way to guarantee that you are able to provide the best teen services possible.

(*Source:* Adapted from Braun, 2011.)

Fear of failure when advocating in general at a level that goes beyond your local community can also be a challenge when going to the larger stage for teen library services advocacy efforts. Keep in mind that in every activity, not just large-arena advocacy activities, there is a chance that something won't go right. Mistakes will probably happen, but it won't be the end of world. Actually, by making mistakes in larger-scale advocacy activities, you'll probably gain insight and experience that will make you more successful the next time. If you acknowledge the fact that you are likely to make mistakes, and use the mistakes you do make to do better next time, there is no reason to fear failure. You can embrace it.

I'm In, Now What?

There are many opportunities to get involved in broad-arena advocacy activities. The following provides a snapshot of what you might check out and participate in.

Associations

Library associations at the regional, state, and national levels are a very good entry point for teen services–related advocacy activities. States around the country have library associations, and many of them are involved in library-related advocacy endeavors, either through an advocacy member group or through their youth services–focused member groups. State associations are an excellent way to get involved in advocacy efforts that take you out of your local comfort zone. They provide an environment where you can connect with like-minded people who also are working with the same state-level budgets and priorities.

At the national level, library organizations such as YALSA, AASL (American Association of School Librarians), ALSC (Association for Library Service to Children), and PLA (Public Library Association) provide opportunities for their members to get involved in activities that are advocacy related. While these activities are national in focus, they often allow for a diversity of ways to get involved. These might include participating on a committee or task force charged with advocating for youth-related library services, blogging or posting on social media, and/or speaking at conferences and events either face-to-face or virtually.

Keep in mind that there are also a variety of associations that are not specifically library focused, but that give you a chance to advocate for teens and teen library services. For example, ISTE (International Society for Technology in Education) and NAA (National Afterschool Association) both have advocacy-related initiatives that connect to, and overlap with, the types of advocacy efforts in which library associations are involved. Expanding to associations outside of the library world makes it possible to speak up and out to members of these associations as well as to the general community to which the association is advocating.

District Days

What are District Days? These are the days (in the late summer) when congressional leaders are back in their districts and not spending time in Washington. They are the days when these leaders sponsor and/or attend events that give them the chance to connect with their constituents. They are the days when teen services library staff can meet face-to-face with legislators to speak up and out about the value of teen library services.

In spring and summer 2011, the YALSA Legislation Committee published a series of articles on the *YALSA Blog* that focused on District Days. The entire series is well worth reading (see Advocacy Resources in Chapter 7 for the full list of posts). You can get started by reading the article from August 2011 that focuses on the top ten reasons for participating in District Days (see the Top Ten Reasons sidebar, pp. 79–80).

State Library Legislative Days

States around the country hold library legislative day events. These events usually take place between January and June each year and center on librarians from across a state joining together, traveling to the Capitol, and visiting the offices of state legislators (American Library Association, 2011). The librarians go out in force to speak up and out about the importance of libraries within a community and a state. It's important that during state library legislative days teen library services voices are heard and the value of libraries in teen lives is recognized. That's why you want to think about getting involved in the legislative day in your state.

As mentioned in Chapter 5, you might bring teens to your state's library legislative day to make sure their voices are heard directly by legislators. Or, you could make sure that a group of teen services librarians from across the state all go to the event and visit legislative offices together with a united message. You and other teen services staff from around your state could:

- Begin (a few months before the event) to craft a plan for getting your message out during the state's library legislative day.

Top Ten Reasons Why Every Library Should Contact Their Local Legislator's Office During District Days

It's almost time for District Days! For those that don't know, District Days refers to the time that congressional representatives are on recess and are able to return to their home district. This year, the break is from August 8th through September 5th. During this time, representatives often hold town hall meetings, office hours, and meet with a variety of constituents to get their perspectives on current issues.

Here Are the Top Ten Reasons Why Every Librarian Should Contact Their Local Legislator's Office During District Days:

10. This is your chance to educate elected officials about a particular area of interest that you have in common.

9. Keeping advocacy efforts at the forefront right now is very important in this tough economy.

8. It is easy! YALSA provides a Legislative Advocacy Guide (http://www.ala.org/ala/mgrps/divs/yalsa/profdev/LegAdvocacyGuide.pdf) with information on how to request a meeting and what to say.

7. Get involved! As librarians we are responsible for the promotion of the interests of the library profession and to speak on behalf of library patrons, especially teens.

6. District Days can help increase appreciation of your library's work, tell your legislators about your library's activities/assistance/programs/needs/etc. in your community.

5. It is a great time to show off your library. In today's tough economy, libraries offer free resources to help people find jobs and learn new skills. Provide to your elected officials stats, use examples, and show how the budget/laws/etc. hurts or helps or changes things.

4. District Days can garner respect for your staff's knowledge of the community, its needs, and assets.

(Continued)

**Top Ten Reasons Why Every Library Should
Contact Their Local Legislator's Office
During District Days** *(Continued)*

3. People of all ages and backgrounds find entertainment, develop skills
   and come to find their place in the community @ the library—tell someone about it!

2. District Days offers the chance to strengthen relations with elected
   officials and/or their staff who may not be very familiar with the work
   of libraries.

And the number one reason Why Every Librarian Should Contact Their Local
Legislator's Office During District Days is:

1. Be a library champion and invest in your library—if you don't, who will?

To find out where your legislator's local office is and how to contact them, visit
CapWiz (http://capwiz.com/ala/home/). Enter your zip code in the box toward the
lower right of the screen, and your Congressional representatives will appear on
the next screen along with contact information for their local and Washington, DC,
offices.

(*Source:* YALSA Legislation Committee, 2011.)

- Work on the message you want to send to legislators. Develop a
  slogan, an elevator pitch, and keywords and phrases that you want to
  get across while talking with legislative staff and officials.

- Determine which key officials you want to talk face-to-face with and
  decide if certain members of the group should take the lead in speaking up and speaking out.

- Develop materials such as infographics (see Chapter 3) on the importance of teen services that you could leave with the legislators.

- Work virtually and/or face-to-face to prepare for your time at library
  legislative day in your state.

Whether you are going to your state's library legislative day as part of a
group or on your own, plan for your participation in the event. Be ready
with your message so that you aren't caught off guard when a legislator or

legislative staffer asks you for information or gives you the opportunity to speak up about library teen services.

National Library Legislative Day

You may get your feet wet at legislative-related advocacy with your state's library legislative day, or you might jump right into National Library Legislative Day (NLLD), which is held each spring in Washington, DC. NLLD brings together librarians from across the United States who meet with legislators on Capitol Hill to talk about library issues and to advocate for the value of libraries in the community. As with state library legislative days, it's imperative that teen services and teens are represented at NLLD.

You can use the same preparation techniques for NLLD as you would for your state's library legislative day. Know that you don't have to attend the event on your own. In fact, many states have groups of librarians travel together to the event and schedule legislative meetings with staffers and legislators which the state's group members attend together. If you are a part of the larger group from your state, get involved in the planning of the group's schedule and message. Doing so can help guarantee that teens and teen library services are part of the message that's sent from the group while talking to legislators and their staff during the day. You might offer to help craft materials that will be made available by the state group for those they visit on Capitol Hill.

NLLD is a very good way to get involved in library advocacy activities at both the state and national levels. You will have the chance to work and network with others from your state who are passionate about libraries, and you will have the opportunity to talk to the officials who make policy at the national level. It's two birds and one stone.

You can find resources that cover state and national library legislative day activities in Chapter 7.

Don't Let Fear Get in the Way

It can be scary to think about speaking up and out for teens outside of your own community. But if you let go of the fear and focus on the benefits to teens in your local area, to libraries in your local area, and to a larger group of teens and libraries across the country, you will see that taking the national, state, or regional advocacy stage is well worth it. As Krista McKenzie (2009) wrote in a *YALSA Blog* article, "Overall, think about the words of Ambrose Redmoon: 'Courage is not the absence of fear, but rather the judgement that something else is more important than fear.' Library and teen advocacy is so important, don't let your fears be your downfall. Turn them around and use them as your stepping stone to advocacy!"

References

American Library Association. 2011. "Legislative Days." ALA Chapters, last modified July 18. http://cro.ala.org/chapters/index.php?title= Legislative_Days.

Braun, Linda. 2011. "Advocacy and Lobbying—What's the Difference?" *YALSA Blog*, October 4. http://yalsa.ala.org/blog/2011/10/04/advocacy-and-lobbying-whats-the-difference/.

Connecticut Association of Nonprofits. 2003. "Advocacy vs. Lobbying: Coalition Building and Public Engagement." Connecticut Association for Nonprofits, revised April 4, http://www.ctnonprofits.org/ctnonprofits/sites/default/files/fckeditor/file/policy/resources/AdvocacyVsLobbying.pdf.

McKenzie, Krista. 2009. "28 Days of Advocacy #19—Overcoming the Fear." *YALSA Blog*, February 19. http://yalsa.ala.org/blog/2009/02/19/28-days-of-advocacy-19-overcoming-the-fear/.

Valenza, Joyce. 2010. "A Nation without School Libraries: Shonda's Crisis Map." *School Library Journal*, March 27. http://blog.schoollibraryjournal.com/neverendingsearch/2010/03/27/a-nation-without-school-librarians-shondas-crisis-map-2/.

YALSA Legislation Committee. 2011. "Top 10 Reasons Why Every Librarian Should Contact Their Local Legislator's Office During District Days." *YALSA Blog*, August 3. http://yalsa.ala.org/blog/2011/08/03/top-ten-reasons-why-every-librarian-should-contact-their-local-legislator%E2%80%99s-office-during-district-days/.

7

Tools for Being a Strong Advocate

40 Developmental Assets® for Adolescents (ages 12 to 18)

External	Support	1. Family support—Family life provides high levels of love and support.
		2. Positive family communication—Young person and her or his parent(s) communicate positively, and young person is willing to seek advice and counsel from parents.
		3. Other adult relationships—Young person receives support from three or more nonparent adults.
		4. Caring neighborhood—Young person experiences caring neighbors.
		5. Caring school climate—School provides a caring, encouraging environment.
		6. Parent involvement in schooling—Parent(s) are actively involved in helping young person succeed in school.
	Empowerment	7. Community values youth—Young person perceives that adults in the community value youth.
		(Continued)

**40 Developmental Assets® for Adolescents
(ages 12 to 18)** *(Continued)*

External *(Continued)*	Empowerment *(Continued)*	8. Youth as resources—Young people are given useful roles in the community.
		9. Service to others—Young person serves in the community one hour or more per week.
		10. Safety—Young person feels safe at home, school, and in the neighborhood.
	Boundaries and Expectations	11. Family boundaries—Family has clear rules and consequences and monitors the young person's whereabouts.
		12. School boundaries—School provides clear rules and consequences.
		13. Neighborhood boundaries—Neighbors take responsibility for monitoring young people's behavior.
		14. Adult role models—Parent(s) and other adults model positive, responsible behavior.
		15. Positive peer influence—Young person's best friends model responsible behavior.
		16. High expectations—Both parent(s) and teachers encourage the young person to do well.
	Constructive Use of Time	17. Creative activities—Young person spends three or more hours per week in lessons or practice in music, theater, or other arts.

(Continued)

40 Developmental Assets® for Adolescents (ages 12 to 18) *(Continued)*

External *(Continued)*	Constructive Use of Time *(Continued)*	18. Youth programs—Young person spends three or more hours per week in sports, clubs, or organizations at school and/or in the community.
		19. Religious community—Young person spends one or more hours per week in activities in a religious institution.
		20. Time at home—Young person is out with friends "with nothing special to do" two or fewer nights per week.
Internal	Commitment to Learning	21. Achievement motivation—Young person is motivated to do well in school.
		22. School engagement—Young person is actively engaged in learning.
		23. Homework—Young person reports doing at least one hour of homework every school day.
		24. Bonding to school—Young person cares about her or his school.
		25. Reading for pleasure—Young person reads for pleasure three or more hours per week.
	Positive Values	26. Caring—Young person places high value on helping other people.
		27. Equality and social justice—Young person places high value on promoting equality and reducing hunger and poverty.

(Continued)

40 Developmental Assets® for Adolescents (ages 12 to 18) *(Continued)*

Internal *(Continued)*	Positive Values *(Continued)*	28. Integrity—Young person acts on convictions and stands up for her or his beliefs.
		29. Honesty—Young person "tells the truth even when it is not easy."
		30. Responsibility—Young person accepts and takes personal responsibility.
		31. Restraint—Young person believes it is important not to be sexually active or to use alcohol or other drugs.
	Social Competencies	32. Planning and decision making—Young person knows how to plan ahead and make choices.
		33. Interpersonal competence—Young person has empathy, sensitivity, and friendship skills.
		34. Cultural competence—Young person has knowledge of and comfort with people of different cultural/racial/ethnic backgrounds.
		35. Resistance skills—Young person can resist negative peer pressure and dangerous situations.
		36. Peaceful conflict resolution—Young person seeks to resolve conflict nonviolently.
	Positive Identity	37. Personal power—Young person feels he or she has control over "things that happen to me."

(Continued)

**40 Developmental Assets® for Adolescents
(ages 12 to 18)** *(Continued)*

Internal *(Continued)*	Positive Identity *(Continued)*	38. Self-esteem—Young person reports having a high self-esteem. 39. Sense of purpose—Young person reports that "my life has a purpose." 40. Positive view of personal future—Young person is optimistic about her or his personal future.

Source: Search Institute, 2007. "40 Developmental Assets for Adolescents." Search Institute. http://www.search-institute.org/content/40-developmental-assets-adolescents-ages-12-18. The list of 40 Development Assets® is reprinted with permission from Search Institute®. Copyright © 1997, 2006 Search Institute, 615 First Avenue NE, Minneapolis, MN 55413. All rights reserved. The following are registered trademarks of Search Institute: Search Institute®, Developmental Assets®, Healthy Communities • Healthy Youth®, and ParentFurther®.

Marketing or Advocacy: You Decide

In Chapter 1 (pp. 3–4), you were asked to determine if the activities listed were advocacy activities, marketing activities, both, or neither. Following is the answer key with an explanation of the answers provided.

1. The library website features information about teen library programs that includes the date and time and a short description. Is this:

   X Marketing   ❏ Both

   ❏ Advocacy   ❏ Neither

   Why did you make that selection?

   _____

   _____

   _____

   _____

This activity is solely a marketing activity. It simply informs members of the community about the existence of the programs. It doesn't explain why the programs are important to teens, or help those visiting the site understand the value that libraries provide by sponsoring this type of program for teens.

2. The director of the library mentions at a meeting of town managers that the library is collecting information and data on the need for a teen-only space in the library. Is this:

X Marketing   ❏ Both

❏ Advocacy   ❏ Neither

Why did you make that selection?

_____

_____

_____

_____

At the base level, this is a marketing activity because the director simply mentions that the data collecting is going on. He or she informs other town managers about the data gathering but doesn't explain why it is important to have the data and how the provision of teen space allows the library to play an important role in teen development. It is possible that this could turn into an advocacy activity if town managers begin to ask the director questions about the data collection and the reasons why the director thinks teen space is important to have. If this happens, the director has a great opportunity to advocate for the role of library teen services in the successful development of adolescents.

3. The teen librarian speaks at a high school PTA meeting about the library collection for teens. She discusses what's in the collection, why different types of materials are purchased, and how the materials help teens to grow up successfully. Is this:

❏ Marketing   ❏ Both

X Advocacy   ❏ Neither

Why did you make that selection?

_____

_____

_____

_____

The teen librarian is not just saying we want teens to have these materials to have access to books that they will enjoy. She is speaking to the reasons beyond pleasure reading for materials in the collection and draws connections between youth development and the collection. Members of the PTA gain an understanding that the library teen collection is developed with thought and care about how the materials support teen needs. As a result, the library teen collection is viewed as a valuable part of the library and the community.

4. A group of teens is talking about the fun they have when taking part in library programs. Is this:

X Marketing   ❏ Both

❏ Advocacy   ❏ Neither

Why did you make that selection?

_____

_____

_____

_____

It's not a bad thing that teens think of the library programs that they go to as fun. Librarians want teens to have fun at their programs. However, when adults in the community, or even peers of the teens, hear only that programs are fun, there is no chance to learn about why the programs that the library provides are worth funding. Teens can have fun at other events that the library doesn't have any hand in sponsoring. That's why when talking about library programs for teens, in order to advocate for those programs, it is essential to bring out why and how the programs are important to a teen's growth and discuss how they support a teen's informational, educational, and personal needs.

5. The mayor meets with members of the press with an update on various activities going on in community departments and agencies. He mentions that the library is expanding their technology access for teens and includes information on why this access will support transliteracy skills.

❑ Marketing   X Both

❑ Advocacy   ❑ Neither

Why did you make that selection?

_____

_____

_____

_____

What a great mayor. Not only does he highlight the library in his comments but he is also advocating for the library and what they do for teens. This is an advocacy endeavor because the mayor goes beyond simply saying the access is available; he explains why that access is important. As a result of his explanation, he is likely to help listeners understand the role the library plays in the community and also gain support for technology access for teens in the library.

Advocacy Skills/Knowledge/Ability Checklist

This checklist is provided as a way to assess where your skills, knowledge, and abilities lie within an advocacy framework. You don't have to have each and every item listed. For those that you don't have, consider who else in your library and/or community has the skills that you are missing. Then think about the ways you can work with the people who have the skills you lack. These individuals can help you gain the skills you need or they can get involved in your advocacy effort so that they bring to the endeavor what you cannot.

Advocacy Skills/Knowledge/Ability Checklist	
Skill/Knowledge/Ability	**Do you have?**
Writing: Print such as newspaper articles and letters to the editor	❑ Yes ❑ No
Writing: Web such as blog posts and articles	❑ Yes ❑ No
Writing: Advertising such as slogan and message development	❑ Yes ❑ No
Presentation: Able to speak in front of a small group to advocate for teen library services	❑ Yes ❑ No
Presentation: Able to speak in front of a large group to advocate for teen library services	❑ Yes ❑ No
Presentation: Able to create dynamic presentations using technology beyond traditional PowerPoint slides	❑ Yes ❑ No
Social media: Understanding of how to use social tools to get a message out and to gain support and interaction with a community	❑ Yes ❑ No
Networking: Comfortable with contacting people in the community to advocate for teen library services	❑ Yes ❑ No
Networking: Know many stakeholders in the community who can support advocacy efforts	❑ Yes ❑ No
Listening: Have an ability to listen closely to what others say, analyze their knowledge of teen library services, and from that listening respond successfully	❑ Yes ❑ No
	(Continued)

Advocacy Skills/Knowledge/Ability Checklist *(Continued)*

Skill/Knowledge/Ability	Do you have?
Knowledge of:	
Adolescent development	❏ Yes ❏ No
Research on teens and technology	❏ Yes ❏ No
Transliteracy	❏ Yes ❏ No
Teen space use and design	❏ Yes ❏ No
Collection development—fiction	❏ Yes ❏ No
Collection development—nonfiction	❏ Yes ❏ No
Collection development—e-content	❏ Yes ❏ No
Marketing to teens	❏ Yes ❏ No
Youth participation	❏ Yes ❏ No
Self-confidence: Able to speak up and out no matter who the audience or what the location	❏ Yes ❏ No
Flexible: Able to go with the flow, change the message, and work through problems when unexpected events and situations arise	❏ Yes ❏ No
Evaluation: Know how to analyze previous advocacy efforts to determine what worked and didn't work and make changes in order to be more successful next time	❏ Yes ❏ No
Risk-friendly: Willingness to try things out even if the outcome is not clear and take on advocacy opportunities that might lead to unexpected results or consequences	❏ Yes ❏ No

Advocacy Resources

American Library Association. 2011. "Add It Up: Libraries Make a Difference in Youth Development and Education, Teens 13-18." American Library Association. Accessed October 31. http://www.ala.org/ala/issuesadvocacy/advleg/advocacyuniversity/additup/13to18/index.cfm.

American Library Association. 2011. "Legislative Action Center." American Library Association. http://capwiz.com/ala/home/.

Flowers, Sarah. 2010. *Young Adults Deserve the Best: YALSA's Competencies in Action*. Chicago: American Library Association/Young Adult Library Services Association.

Gallaway, Beth. 2010. "Make It Count: Advocacy and Teen Read Week." *Young Adult Library Services* 8, no. 4: 24–28.

Illinois Library Association and the American Library Association. 2004. "Library Advocacy." Illinois Library Association. http://www.ila.org/pdf/advocacy.pdf.

International Federation of Library Associations and Institutions. 2006. "School Library Resource Centers Section: School Library Advocacy Kit." IFLA. Revised July 28. http://archive.ifla.org/VII/s11/pubs/s11_AdvocacyKit.html.

LaRue, James. 2011. "Keeping Our Message Simple." *American Libraries* 42, no. 5/6. http://americanlibrariesmagazine.org/features/06082011/keeping-our-message-simple.

Public Library Association. 2007. *Libraries Prosper with Passion, Purpose, and Persuasion: A PLA Toolkit for Success*. Chicago: Public Library Association.

Scordato, Julie. 2010. "Advocacy Mechanics with Mary Arnold." *VOYA* 33, no. 2: 135.

Young Adult Library Services Association. 2012. "Advocating for Teen Services in Libraries." Young Adult Library Services Association. Last modified January 18. http://wikis.ala.org/yalsa/index.php/Advocating_for_Teen_Services_in_Libraries.

Young Adult Library Services Association. 2012. *YALSA Blog*, Advocacy category. Young Adult Library Services Association. Accessed January 25. http://yalsa .ala.org/blog/category/advocacy/.

The Importance of a Whole Library Approach to Public Library Young Adult Services: A YALSA Issue Paper

Written for YALSA by Linda W. Braun with contributions from Sarah Flowers and Mary Hastler

Adopted by YALSA's Board of Directors, January 8, 2011

Introduction

It is crucial that all library staff have the skills and knowledge necessary to serve the young adult population with respect and first-rate services. When all public libraries are fully staffed only with those who value young adults, not only does the library thrive, but the community, of which adolescents are a part, thrives as well.

When an adolescent walks into a library he or she may use any number of the services available. A 17-year-old customer may visit the library's technology center in order to locate information about jobs that are available after graduation from high school. A 15-year-old student might seek help from reference staff to complete a research paper on the causes of the French revolution. It is essential that these young adults receive the information-seeking assistance required from well-trained and respectful staff. When they do, the library provides the value that the community deserves.

Abstract

Any community member who walks into a public library or visits a library website should expect the highest quality of service available. This is no truer for children than it is for adults, and no truer for adults than it is for young adults. In some communities, teens are relegated to a specific area of the library with the hope that they will stay there, and that the one staff member assigned to work with teens will keep anyone in that age group out of the way of everyone else. Appropriate and attractive space for teens to read, do homework, and socialize is important but teens also need to feel welcome in all areas of the library.

It is important when promoting positive adolescent development for teens that the age group be treated equitably—and teens know when there is a service double standard in place. As a result, teens sometimes choose to exhibit undesirable behaviors or choose to no longer use the institution that they perceive as treating them inappropriately. The ramifications on the library can be long term as support from future taxpayers is potentially lost. Teens may also fight back with displays of inappropriate behavior while in the library and these can extend into the local community.

Adolescence is a confusing time for many teens and as a result it is also turbulent for those around them. Young adults are grown but not fully grown. Teenagers can act like adults one minute and like children the next. It's sometimes hard to know what to expect, which is one of the reasons why many adults are wary around the age group.

This dynamic does not have to exist and it can be changed by providing young adults in the library with a full complement of services and staff who have the skills and knowledge necessary to serve the age group. This can be accomplished through staff professional development, collaboration, and administrative support.

Problem Statement

Young adult service staffing models in public libraries across the United States vary widely. Examples include libraries with:

- no staff members assigned responsibilities that focus on services to adolescents
- staff with primary responsibilities in children's or adult areas that are also asked to provide services to teens on an ad hoc basis
- a staff member that is designated as a part-time teen services librarian while also responsible for at least one other area of library services to a different population group
- a staff member that is a designated full-time teen services librarian
- staff that make up a full teen department with full-time and part-time members directly (and only) assigned to serving teens

The ideal in any library is to have at least one full-time young adult librarian and to have all staff throughout the library fully understand the developmental needs of young adults and possess the skills necessary to serve teens successfully. This ideal has proved hard to achieve. In their

2007 study, the Public Library Association found that only 51 percent of public libraries have a full-time young adults services librarian. Sixty-two percent of these libraries have at least one staff person whose job it is specifically to serve teens. This is an improvement over figures from 1994, which indicated that only 11 percent of public libraries had a staff person whose job it was to serve teens. Still, there is plenty of room for improvement.

Many libraries have staff in non-teen departments who are wary of adolescents and/or choose to have nothing to do with the age group. In many of these libraries administration, for whatever reason, does not stand up for teenagers as a unique age group and require that all staff provide the age group with high-quality service.

Recognizing that not all teen services specialists (along with library staff members who are not teen services specialists but yet interact with teens on a regular basis) are able to keep up with teen-related research and skills, in 1996 YALSA launched the Serving the Underserved program. This initiative provided train-the-trainer professional development to librarians across the United States. This training enabled trainees to take their learning back into their own communities and assist colleagues and peers in providing better service to adolescents. Overall, the program laid the groundwork for supporting staff not specifically trained to work with young adults so that all library staff members could serve the age group successfully.

At the time that YALSA initiated the Serving the Underserved program, libraries around the country started to recognize the importance of teen services. This acknowledgment is seen in the growth of YALSA, which in the mid-to-late 2000s saw strong increases in membership and this growth led to the Association's becoming the fastest growing division of the American Library Association (ALA).

A factor leading to the increased recognition of young adults in libraries was the sheer number of teenagers in the United States. Census figures released in 2008 show that there were close to 42 million young adults in the United States. This large number of adolescents, along with the burgeoning of social media use by teens, the surge in the quantity of information available to young adults in print and on the web, and the significant growth of publishing in young adult literature, led to acknowledgment by some librarians that young adults require a full complement of high-quality library services in order to support their use of and access to a variety of technologies and print resources.

Research on teens and their developmental needs and behaviors is a growing field as researchers seek data on the impact on new technologies on the teenage brain. In November 2010, Harvard researcher, Dr. Frances Jensen, spoke to neuroscientists about scientific findings that demonstrate the brain is only 80 percent developed when a child reaches adolescence (Juskalian, 2010). These findings are an important part of this discussion because they point to the need for librarians to not make assumptions about young adult abilities and knowledge. While teens have brains that are more developed than those of children, young adults don't have the brain of a fully developed adult. As a result, sometimes teens require support from children's services staff and sometimes they require support from those primarily tasked with serving adults. And, there are times when a young adult services librarian is exactly what an adolescent needs. Adolescents are grown but not fully grown and as such need to have library services that support their needs as developing adults who must make use of children's, young adult, and adult library programs and services.

Proposed Solution

In 2010 YALSA updated its "Competencies for Librarians Serving Youth: Young Adults Deserve the Best" and added a companion book and evaluation tool to the suite of competency materials available. This update and expansion increased the number of resources available that aid state level library agency staff, administrators, and frontline librarians in development of high-quality teen library services and the evaluation and measurement of these services. The Communication, Marketing, and Outreach section of the competencies states, "The librarian will be able to establish an environment in the library wherein all staff serve young adults with courtesy and respect, and all staff are encouraged to promote programs and services for young adults." This statement highlights the value of providing young adult services outside of the isolated framework of a sole teen librarian being the only staff member that is knowledgeable about, and providing services to, the age group.

Anyone spending time in a public library will quickly see how frequently young adults use all aspects of library services. For example, teens:

- Repeatedly require assistance and support from reference staff to locate homework materials and materials that support personal information needs.

- Need to discuss borrowing records with circulation staff.

- Use computers and other technologies for reading, writing, communicating, collaborating, and creating and often need the support of information technology staff as they work on projects in these areas.

- Take part in events and programs sponsored by agencies with which library outreach staff collaborates.

- Spend time in the children's, teen, and adult departments in order to locate materials or to help out with programs.

How can all library staff support young adults who use a wide variety of library spaces and resources?

Staff Training and Professional Development

A library with a strong commitment to young adults guarantees that the age group is treated with respect by the entire library staff. This is possible only when all staff take part in training related to the developmental assets of teens. Knowledge of these assets, and of why they are important to the successful growth of adolescents, provides library staff with a foundation from which to work when developing policies, collections and programs. This knowledge also provides an understanding of why teens behave as they do when inside a library as well as a comprehension of how to react to sometimes challenging young adult behaviors.

Collaboration in Collection Development

Young adult services staff, reference staff, and children's services staff must work together to plan for collections that not only support the homework help needs of young adults, but also meet the personal information needs of the age group. Both male and female adolescents require opportunities to access materials such as those that support their personal interests from learning about relationships, to discovering options for life after high school, to finding out about current trends in entertainment or fashion. A full complement of materials such as magazines and books in the adult, teen, and children's areas of the library are required in order to support the educational, recreational, and personal growth needs of teens at all levels of development.

Information Literacy Support Across Library Departments

Data released by the Pew Internet and American Life Project in February 2010 found that "Teens continue to be avid users of social networking websites—as of September 2009, 73% of online American teens ages 12 to 17 used an online social network website, a statistic that has continued to climb upwards from 55% in November 2006 and 65% in February 2008" (Lenhart et al., 2010). This high rate of young adult use of virtual social networking points to the need for technology, reference, and teen services staff to work together to develop face-to-face and virtual programs that support teens' information literacy needs and their need to learn to be safe and smart when communicating and collaborating in virtual environments.

Programming for Parents Regarding Adolescence and Adolescent Trends

Technology, adult services, children's services, and teen services staff also play a part in educating parents, teachers, and others about the role technology plays in the lives of teens. Many adults who live and work with teens do not have a firm understanding of the why and how of teen technology use, particularly use related to social media and interactive technologies (often referred to as Web 2.0). Education by librarians on this topic helps adults better understand young adult interests and behaviors within the social media arena.

Similarly, parents are not always secure in their understanding of the changes that take place as their children move from childhood to adulthood. Parents may feel comfortable with children's staff after years of bringing their children to programs at the library and these staff can help a parent with learning how to live with a teen. Adult staff may have a rapport with parents with whom they discuss fiction and nonfiction materials checked out of the library. Due to this rapport, these staff members may prove to be the best qualified to help parents find resources that help them to understand the changes a teenage son or daughter is experiencing.

Cross-Generational Mentoring Opportunities

Children's services, adult services, and young adult services staff who work together to plan initiatives that provide teens with opportunities to mentor children and tutor seniors play a significant role in helping young adults gain important developmental assets. The Search Institute's list of assets that teens need in order to grow up successfully includes assets of empowerment, support, and social competencies. Programs in which teens share skills and knowledge with those younger and older are essential in helping teens to gain these assets and therefore play a role in an adolescent's long-term growth and development.

Future Directions

Success in the whole library approach to young adult services will occur with complete support from library administration. Administrators who move forward in this framework will:

- Model for all staff members high-quality librarian and young adult customer service interactions. Not only will these interactions serve as models for staff, they will also demonstrate the administrator's own understanding of teen developmental assets and needs.

- Regularly provide opportunities for all library staff to take part in professional development focusing on techniques for working with adolescents. Continuing education will also be made available on topics related to teen trends in areas including technology, popular culture, information, and social experiences and behaviors.

- Regularly evaluate library services, looking specifically at the quality of teen services across all library departments and communicate with staff to inform them when instances of inadequate service to young adults occur. The administrator will also inform staff that such service is not acceptable in the library.

- Hire only staff that is able to demonstrate the ability to work with young adults no matter what library department is designated as his or her main service area.

- Speak out to community and government agencies, parents, and staff on the value of young adults in the library and in the community as a whole.

Recommendations

The Young Adult Library Services Association asserts that young adult services must be integrated into public libraries as a part of a full continuum of library service. Because adolescents require library services that support unique developmental needs both at the upper and lower ends of the age spectrum, it is crucial that libraries and library staff embrace a whole library approach and integrate teen services into the entire library program including children's, young adult, adult, reference, circulation, technology, and technical services.

Resources

Flowers, Sarah. 2010. *Young Adults Deserve the Best: YALSA's Competencies in Action.* Chicago: American Library Association/Young Adult Library Services Association.

Juskalian, Russ. 2010. "The Kids Can't Help It." *Newsweek*, December 16. http://www.newsweek.com/2010/12/16/the-kids-can-t-help-it.html.

Lenhart, Amanda, Kristen Purcell, Aaron Smith, and Kathryn Zickhuhr. 2010. "Social Media and Young Adults—Part 3: Social Media." *Pew Internet & American Life Project Report*, February 3. http://www.pewinternet.org/Reports/2010/Social-Media-and-Young-Adults/Part-3/1-Teens-and-online-social-networks.aspx.

Public Library Association. 2007. *PLDS Statistical Report.* Chicago: Public Library Association.

Search Institute. 2007. "40 Developmental Assets for Adolescents 12 to 18." Search Institute. http://www.search-institute.org/content/40-developmental-assets-adolescents-ages-12-18.

U.S. Census Bureau. 2008. "Resident Population by Age and Sex: The 2009 Statistical Abstract." U.S. Census Bureau. http://www.census.gov/compendia/statab/cats/population/estimates_and_projections_by_age_sex_raceethnicity.html.

YALSA, with Audra Caplan. 2009. "The Benefits of Including Dedicated Young Adult Librarians on Staff in the Public Library." American Library Association. http://www.ala.org/ala/mgrps/divs/yalsa/profdev/whitepapers/yastaff.cfm.

YALSA. 2010. "YALSA's Competencies for Librarians Serving Youth: Young Adults Deserve the Best." American Library Association. http://www.ala.org/yalsa/competencies.

Index

About the Author and YALSA

Linda W. Braun is an Educational Technology Consultant with LEO: Librarians & Educators Online. She provides training and consulting services to schools, libraries, and other educational institutions on how to integrate technology successfully. Linda was the 2009–2010 president of the Young Adult Library Services Association (YALSA) and served as the association's blog manager from 2006–2009. She is a Professor of Practice for Simmons College Graduate School of Library and Information Science, where she teaches courses on web development, technology, and teen services. Linda has written books for ALA Editions, YALSA, Neal-Schuman, and Information Today and she is a columnist for *VOYA*.

The **Young Adult Library Services Association (YALSA)** is the fourth-largest division of the American Library Association, with more than 5,400 members. YALSA's mission is to expand and strengthen library services for teens and young adults. Through its member-driven advocacy, research, and professional development initiatives, YALSA builds the capacity of libraries and librarians to engage, serve, and empower teens and young adults. YALSA's major initiatives include Teen Read Week™ and Teen Tech Week™. Known as the world leader in recommending books and media to those ages 12–18, YALSA each year gives out six literary awards, including the Printz Award, and chooses titles for seven book and media lists. For more information about YALSA, visit http://www.ala.org/yalsa or http://www.ala.org/yalsa/booklists.